❧ VICIOUS CIRCLE ❧

VICIOUS CIRCLE

*The case of the missing
Irish Crown Jewels*

❧❧❧❧❧❧

Francis Bamford and Viola Bankes

MAX PARRISH · LONDON

MAX PARRISH AND CO LTD
1–5 PORTPOOL LANE
LONDON EC1

MADE AND PRINTED IN GREAT BRITAIN BY
WILLIAM CLOWES & SONS LTD
LONDON AND BECCLES

❧CONTENTS❧

LIST OF PLATES

(between pp. 92–3)

'The detectives might well say that it is an affair for a Sherlock Holmes to investigate.'

Sir Arthur Vicars, in an interview
published in the *Daily Express*,
15th July, 1907

Will anyone ever have the courage to tell the whole truth about this wretched business?

London Mail, 13th November, 1912

FOREWORD

The disappearance of the Irish Crown Jewels in 1907 from the Office of Arms in Dublin Castle remains one of the great unsolved mysteries of this century. No full account of the incident has ever been published; but the details are so curious, the nemesis which pursued almost all those involved in the story so horrifying, that we believe many readers will share our absorbed interest.

The Irish Crown Jewels, or the State Jewels, as Irish officials now prefer to style them, were presented to the Order of St Patrick by King William the Fourth in 1830 to be worn on formal occasions by the Lord-Lieutenant of Ireland as Grand Master of the Order. The Jewels consisted of the Star and Badge of the Order, and are believed to have been formed from some of the diamonds, once the property of Queen Charlotte, which were given by George IV to Lady Conyngham and, after his death, returned by her with unexpected delicacy to his executors.[1]

The Star was of eight points composed of Brazilian diamonds; in the centre a shamrock of emeralds shone from the heart of a ruby cross which lay upon a background of blue enamel. Encircling this central *motif* was the motto of the Order, *Quis Separabit?* and the date MDCCLXXXIII[2] all in rose diamonds. The Badge was of a like splendour, its trefoil of emeralds on a ruby cross being surrounded by a blue enamel band bearing the motto and date in rose diamonds, which was itself enclosed in an outer circle of large Brazilian diamonds, the whole being surmounted by a harp and loop, all formed of diamonds.

Our efforts to unravel the tangled yarns of evidence and narrative were, almost from the beginning, made more difficult by that enveloping cloak of silence with which, for his own mistaken reasons, King Edward the Seventh sought to shroud the whole affair. So efficiently were his wishes carried out that when, in 1912, King George the Fifth suggested that new efforts might

[1] For a full account of this transaction see *The Journal of Mrs Arbuthnot*, by the Duke of Wellington, K.G., and Francis Bamford (Macmillan & Co., London, 1950), App. A., Vol. II, pp. 443–7.

[2] George III established the Order in 1783.

be made to recover the jewels, his royal hopes were almost at once strangled with a web of governmental red tape. Even now, after more than fifty years, the mere mention of the case retains the power of afflicting reputedly intelligent persons with a kind of mass amnesia, rendering them unable to remember anything of events in which they themselves, or their close relatives, were personally involved.

It has even been suggested to us that we should relinquish our task because, it is claimed, the whole matter was finally settled with the publication of the Report drawn up by the Commissioners who, in 1908, inquired into certain aspects of the theft. With respect, and although this Report has provided much of the material for our book, we would suggest that the mystery cannot be regarded as closed satisfactorily until the Jewels are restored to the Sovereign, their rightful owner.

Because of this prevailing reluctance on the part of some to tell us what they know, we are all the more grateful to those who have given so generously of their memories, their time and their assistance. Even some of these have preferred to remain anonymous, and to each one of them, known and unknown, friends and unfriends, we would express the same sense of gratitude and acknowledgment as we do towards the Hon. Lady Meade-Fetherstonhaugh; Sir Anthony Weldon, Bart.; David Anderson, sometime First Secretary at the British Embassy in Dublin; Gerard Slevin, Chief Herald for Ireland; M. R. Trappes-Lomax, Somerset Herald; R. L. Wynn-Williams of the Metropolitan Police Office, New Scotland Yard, London; Séamus O'Farrell (who so kindly lent us the photograph of his mother); to Dr Maud O'Mahony and N. H. Parker, F.L.A., Librarian to Malvern District Council, and to his Staff for the careful and time-consuming researches they made on our behalf. To Basil O'Connell, K.M., we are deeply indebted for permission to use the letters written by Sir Arthur Vicars to Mr James F. Fuller which are now in his possession. To F. Higenbottam, F.L.A., City Librarian of Canterbury, we would express our particular thanks for arranging that we might reproduce the photograph of Francis Bennett-Goldney, and to quote extensively from Mr Stone's article, *An Edwardian Machiavelli*, which appeared in the ninth issue of *Good Books at the Beaney: Quarterly Bulletin of the Canterbury Royal Museum and Public Library*,

Christmas 1949; as also to H. G. Pearson, Departmental Record Officer, Establishment and Organisation Department at the Home Office, for so considerately making it possible for us to inspect and publish extracts from a number of papers connected with the loss of the Crown Jewels. We are also most appreciative of the great help given to us by members of the staff of the British Museum and of the National Libraries of Scotland and of Ireland. To the Director of the latter we are indebted for permission to publish the Chamney Papers now preserved in the Genealogical Office, Dublin Castle. Particular thanks are due to Donogh O'Malley, Parliamentary Secretary to the Minister of Finance, Dublin, for kindly providing the ground plan of the Bedford Tower as it was in 1907; and to Dr Michael Megan for so generously offering the use of his picture by Rose Barton of carriages arriving for a Drawing Room at Dublin Castle; and to Miss Rose Brooke, a niece of the artist, for permission to reproduce this picture.

For permission to use quotations from printed works we are grateful to Sir John Murray, K.C.V.O., D.S.O., in respect of Sir Arthur Conan Doyle's short story *The Bruce-Partington Plans*, which appeared in *His Last Bow* (John Murray, London, 1917): and of Lord Ronald Sutherland-Gower's *Old Diaries* (1902): to the Public Trustee in respect of Sir Sidney Lee's *King Edward VII: A Biography* (Macmillan & Co., London): to Messrs Methuen and Co. in respect of *More Cracks with 'We Twa'* by the first Marquess and Marchioness of Aberdeen and Temair: and to the Syndics of the Fitzwilliam Museum, Cambridge, for permission to publish extracts from Wilfrid Scawen Blunt's *My Diaries* (Martin Secker, London).

Lastly, we would record our gratitude to Sir Arthur Vicars' nephew, Mr. Robert de Janasz, for leave to quote from his uncle's letters; to Eoin O'Mahony, K.M., K.L.J., for his tireless interest and assistance; and to our Irish hosts, to our regret veiled in anonymity, for their generous hospitality in both Dublin and the country. They gave us splendid opportunities to study the Irish scene, the Irish weather and the Irish character. These are things we shall not easily forget.

BOOK ONE

The Disappearance

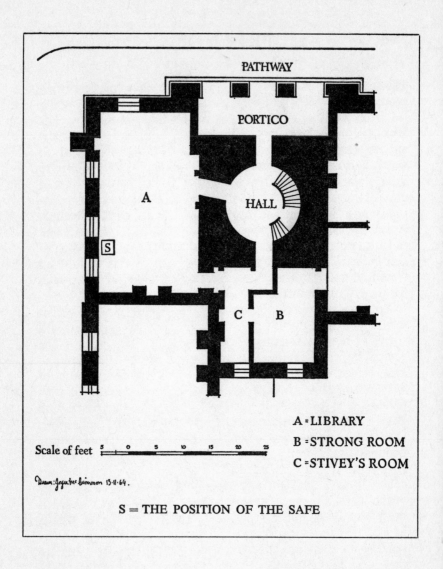

PATHWAY

PORTICO

HALL

A

S

C   B

Scale of feet   5   0   5   10   15   20   25

Drawn: Joyce McSwinnon 13·11·64.

A = LIBRARY
B = STRONG ROOM
C = STIVEY'S ROOM

S = THE POSITION OF THE SAFE

Ground plan of the Office of Arms at Dublin Castle

PRELUDE

The stage was set. It was 4th May, 1907. Since early morning groups of sightseers had been gathering along the roads which led from Dublin to Ballsbridge where, later in the day, His Excellency the Lord-Lieutenant would open the Irish International Exhibition. There was plenty for the spectators to watch and discuss, for the nobility and gentry of Ireland were driving in open carriages towards the Exhibition. Nothing pleased so much the ordinary people of Dublin as an opportunity to polish their native wit at the expense of their betters. And today, since the ladies were draped, swathed and trimmed in yard upon yard of Irish lace – an outward and visible sign of the industries which, the promoters hoped, this Exhibition would do much to foster – the watchers found material enough for their frank and friendly comments.

Within the Exhibition grounds the feverish activity of recent weeks was temporarily stilled, though teams of gardeners still strove to repair the damage wrought by the April storms. The general impression, however, was impressive enough. From the great central hall with its glass dome, almost as large as that of St Paul's Cathedral, radiated four noble galleries filled with telling examples of modern art and industry, interspersed with Napoleonic relics and collections of historic glass and silver. One gallery contained a spectacular display of machinery, manufactured for the most part in England, and some fine Irish-built railway engines and carriages. Another, the art gallery, held what *The Times* correspondent described as 'many of the world's most famous pictures'. King Edward had graciously lent Lady Butler's 'Roll Call', while the Tsar of Russia had carried this somewhat depressing theme a step further by sending an immense canvas entitled 'The Cemetery'. Besides these were examples of the work of Corot, Detaille, Millet, Rosa Bonheur, Poynter, Whistler, Millais and Luke Fildes, while the groups of statuary were as remarkable as were the pictures.

By eleven o'clock all the seats in the Concert Hall were filled, saving only those reserved for the elect who would presently come in procession with the Lord Lieutenant and his Countess. 'Everyone who was anybody in Ireland', declared *The Times*, 'was present ... or sent a message of regret for unavoidable absence.' Nor were the invited guests permitted to find their time of waiting long. Massed beneath the great organ at the upper end of the hall was a choir, 360 strong; and throughout the morning these were led through the first part of the elaborate programme prepared by their conductor, Mr Barton McGuckin.

Shortly before noon, as the music drew to a close, those in the Concert Hall heard the sound of Irish cheers. *They* had arrived after driving in state from Dublin Castle. Now, as the carriage came to a halt before the Grand Entrance, the Marquess of Ormonde, President of the Executive Council, went down the steps to receive the viceregal couple. The members of the procession bridled in their uniforms or morning dress as their time of uneasy waiting drew to an end.

Then, into that silence which so often precedes the arrival of the Great and Good, came Lord Ormonde escorting to their places the Lord-Lieutenant and the Countess of Aberdeen. As the orchestra played selections from *Tannhäuser*, the procession began its slow and fairly stately way towards the Concert Hall. (Not only was there the usual hobble of distinguished veterans, but poor Lady Aberdeen had suffered severely throughout the Season from rheumatic twinges.)

First, two by two, walked the Contractors and Consulting Architects, then the members of the Executive Council of the Exhibition and its estimable Vice-Presidents. The mayors of various Irish towns were followed by representatives of the Colonies and foreign governments, as well as by bemedalled officers from the armed services. Behind these, in a swelling crescendo of ever-increasing importance, came, those who formed the immediate entourage of the Viceroy. Some of these will appear again and again within these pages; but on that May day of brilliant sunshine, glittering uniforms, fashionable toilettes and bearded greatness, none can have guessed that very soon many were to be drawn into a bewildering web of fear and suspicion from which some would never break wholly free.

From this point the printed Order of Procession read:

The Assistant Commissioner	The Chief Commissioner
Dublin Metropolitan Police	Dublin Metropolitan Police
(W. V. Harrel, Esq., M.V.O.)	(Lt-Col Sir John Ross
	of Bladensburg, K.C.B.)

Athlone Pursuivant of Arms
in his Tabard
(F. Bennett-Goldney, Esq.,
F.S.A.)

Cork Herald in his Tabard,
wearing the Collar of S.S.
(P. G. Mahony, Esq.,
M.R.I.A.)[1]

The Knights of St Patrick:

Earl of Mayo, K.P.   Viscount Iveagh, K.P.
Earl of Kilmorey, K.P.   Marquess of Ormonde, K.P.

Dublin Herald in his Tabard,
wearing the Collar of S.S.
(F. R. Shackleton, Esq.)

Asst Private Secretary   Asst Vice-Chamberlain
Asst Under-Secretary   Dean of the Chapel Royal
to the Lord-Lieutenant
(Sir James B. Dougherty,
C.V.O., C.B.)

Private Secretary   Vice-Chamberlain
(The Lord Herschell)   (Sir Anthony Weldon, Bart.,
D.S.O.)

Comptroller   State Steward &
(Viscount Powerscourt,   Chamberlain
M.V.O.)   (Earl of Liverpool, M.V.O.)

Ulster King of Arms in his Tabard,
wearing the Collar of S.S.
(Sir Arthur Vicars, K.C.V.O.)

The Countess of Aberdeen   The Lord-Lieutenant
wearing the Insignia of
Grand Master of the
Order of St Patrick[2]

When Their Excellencies were comfortably settled, Lord Ormonde read an address of welcome. To this, after first reading to his audience a telegram which the King had sent him from Paris, the Lord-Lieutenant was pleased to reply. As a reward he was given, 'as a specimen of Dublin workmanship and art, and a souvenir of this memorable occasion', a singularly useless gift, a golden key without a lock. Lord Aberdeen thereupon thanked the members of the Executive Council for

[1] In the event Mr Mahony was unable to be present, having been taken ill on April 22nd or 23rd.
[2] This was the undress Insignia.

their handsome present and, turning to Ulster King of Arms, a striking figure in his emblazoned tabard, commanded him to declare the Exhibition open. In ringing tones, Ulster cried:

'By command of His Excellency the Lord Lieutenant, I proclaim the Exhibition open.'

As the echo of his words was drowned in a great outburst of applause, which was itself superseded by a flourish of trumpets, no one realised that Sir Arthur Vicars, Ulster King of Arms, had made his last public pronouncement in that ancient and chivalric appointment.

CHAPTER ONE

1 ⚡

Arthur Vicars was born at Leamington in Warwickshire in 1864. His father, a colonel in the 61st Regiment, died when Arthur was only five years old. His mother survived her husband for no more than five years. She had been born a Gun-Cuninghame of Mount Kennedy in County Wicklow, a family descended from members of both the Irish and French nobilities. In 1830 she had married Peirce K. Mahony of Kilmorna and Gunsborough. These Mahonys of Kilmorna, putting their trust in the chastity of countless generations of women, claimed as the founder of their house one Olioll Olum, Ard-ri or High King of Munster in the third century after Christ. Mrs Vicars' sons by her first marriage, George and Peirce, were to play at least as great a part in Arthur's life as did his own brothers and sister; and, though he was educated in England at Magdalen College School, Oxford, and Bromsgrove School, he spent his holidays in the Irish country houses belonging to his stepbrothers. Thus it was that he came to feel for Kilmorna a more enduring love, perhaps, than for anything or anyone else.

When he left school he possessed very little money, a good deal of charm and no prospects. At first it was thought that he should train for the Law, and he began to do so; but, by that good fortune which so often attends those who appear to struggle least for it, his precocious interest in genealogical matters attracted the notice of the aged Sir Bernard Burke, who had been Ulster King of Arms since 1843. Vicars entered the Office of Arms and in 1893, following Sir Bernard's death, was chosen to succeed him. At the age of 29 he was created Ulster King of Arms, Registrar of, and Knight Attendant on, the Order of St Patrick. As Ulster King of Arms he acted, as does Lyon King in Scotland, directly under the Crown and not, as Garter King of Arms in England must, under the Earl Marshal. As an institution the post was comparatively recent, dating only from the reign of King Edward VI; but it is doubtful whether there was any other post in the whole world which could have brought so much satisfaction to Vicars who, by name and birth an Englishman, longed to identify himself with that older Ireland of which his stepbrothers were representative.

His patent of appointment stated that the King of Arms should hold office while he was of good behaviour and at the Sovereign's pleasure. This wording can never have given rise, either in his own mind or in those of his friends, to the least qualm of uneasiness. Arthur Vicars appeared to possess in full measure that quality of discretion which is the hallmark of a successful courtier.

Thus, as Ulster King of Arms answerable only to the Sovereign and his own conscience as to whom he might or might not admit to the ranks of the Irish gentry, his mind engrossed in the finical details of quarterings and co-heirs, of bars of bastardy and escutcheons of honour, Vicars withdrew into a world of heraldry, an exact science based upon purely artificial premises. For him this appointment was a triumph of poetry over prose, as well as an answer to the increasingly pressing problem of how he was to contrive to live as a gentleman and a connoisseur.

Throughout his life, when he was in a position to do so, Vicars collected fine books and old silver. In the homes of his Irish relatives and friends he had absorbed those standards of good taste which flowered so splendidly in the great houses of eighteenth-century Ireland: and thus, most probably from the start, he began to live beyond his means. In this he was, of course, far from unique. The possession of informed taste almost always leads those fortunates who have it into financial difficulties, which are only partially palliated by the bitter-sweet knowledge that it is in the remembrance of their economies rather than of their extravagances that they find reason for regret.

At this stage, however, he was far from being worried. He wanted only to make his office as efficient as possible. With this object in view, he appointed as Secretary to the Office of Arms Mr George Dames Burtchaell, a distinguished genealogist and, for many years, a member of the Irish Bar. In choosing Mr Burtchaell, Vicars displayed a wisdom which was, regrettably, all too often lacking at other times. The Secretary, a man of common sense and solid worth, proved an invaluable colleague, supplying a method of work and power of decision which Vicars did not himself possess. The only drawback was that Burtchaell was subject to epileptic fits.

Life adopted a quiet and agreeable pattern for Vicars, with only occasional highlights such as, when Queen Victoria paid her last visit to Ireland, he displayed to his Sovereign, pushed in a wicker Bath chair, the Crown Jewels. Again, after the Queen's death, he played his expected part at the coronation of King Edward.

Then, on 29th July, 1905, the revised statutes of the Order of St Patrick were promulgated. Under the new constitution of the Order, Vicars was to hold his appointment for life, so long as he was of good behaviour. It was also decreed that the posts of various heralds and junior pursuivants, which had been allowed to lapse, were to be revived. Vicars was delighted at this, because it provided him with the opportunity to show in a practical way his gratitude to two young men who had, although they held no official post, helped him with the work of the Office.

One of these was his nephew, Peirce Gun Mahony, at this time 27 years of age and married to a charming and intelligent Englishwoman, Ethel Tindall Wright, the younger daughter of a Yorkshire doctor. Young Mahony had for long been a close friend of his uncle; and Vicars now bestowed upon him the post of Cork Herald. The appointment carried no salary, but it would secure for his nephew a place in the world of official Dublin. He thought, too, that this would be some small return for all the kindness he had received from Peirce's father. It was typical of Vicars that he should never have considered whether his stepbrother, an ardent Nationalist, would approve of his elder son becoming a member of the Viceroy's staff. But the elder Peirce was furious. There was a violent and prolonged quarrel between the two stepbrothers and, presumably, between father and son, because the younger Mahony continued to act as Cork Herald. But Vicars, though hurt by what he regarded as his brother's unreasonable attitude, could not be for long cast down. Political considerations must not be allowed to interfere with the plans he had made for the composition of his small heraldic court.

He recommended that the office of Dublin Herald should be conferred upon his friend, Francis Richard Shackleton, the son of an Irish doctor who had, before the birth of his younger son, forsaken the beauties of County Kildare for the more lucrative, but infinitely less romantic, neighbourhood of Dulwich. Vicars had first met Shackleton in 1897 when the latter was hoping to find employment in the College of Arms in London and had written to Vicars on some genealogical matters. The job had failed to materialise and, in October, 1899, Vicars offered him the post of assistant to Mr Burtchaell. Shackleton accepted, but the arrangement must have been of short duration. The outbreak of the South African War brought to the colours almost every flower of British youth. Shackleton was commissioned in the 3rd Battalion, Royal Irish Fusiliers, as from 23rd October, 1900, and sailed for South Africa early in the New Year. His term of service there was brief, for he was invalided home in August, 1901, after being awarded the Queen's Medal, with clasp. He left the army in February, 1903, with a disability pension which he continued to draw until his death. In 1903, when Vicars was making the arrangements for King Edward's visit to Ireland, he invited Shackleton to serve as a Gold Staff Officer. Now he made him Dublin Herald.

The young man was delighted. This was just such a distinction as he needed at that time when he set out to conquer London Society as a prelude to gaining the fortune he planned to make. His term of military service seems to have brought him a considerable measure of worldly wisdom. Not only did he realise now the full value of the very remarkable assets with which he had been endowed at birth, but he also understood that this appointment would serve to stress his Irish ancestry, which was far more interesting than claiming merely to have been born almost within the translucent shadow of the Crystal Palace.

His appearance in London was noted with approval by more than one section of the brilliant, glittering world of Edwardian Society. A friend who knew him at that time has written of him as being 'extremely good-looking and extremely depraved'. His success and advancement appeared to be assured. Obtaining a post with a firm of brokers in the City, he soon showed that, in addition to his other gifts, he possessed the ability to work hard.

When, in 1905, he became Dublin Herald, he was regarded in London as a coming man; and, two years later, he was a member of no less than four London clubs and the tenant of a bachelor flat at 44 Park Lane. It is scarcely surprising that the mantelpiece in his sitting-room became daily more difficult to dust as the drift of invitations upon it grew ever deeper.

At the time this story opens, Shackleton had helped to launch a company which, having acquired the option on an immense tract of forest land in Mexico, stood to make spectacular profits for those concerned in it. He possessed a zest for living, an effervescent optimism which made him believe that Eldorado lay only just round the next corner; and Vicars was charmed with these traits, so totally dissimilar to his own characteristics.

It was not long after Shackleton's appointment as Dublin Herald that he and Vicars decided to set up house together, although it was understood that Shackleton's business activities would make it impossible for him to spend much time in Ireland. So Vicars disposed of his house in Wellington Road and moved to 7 St James's Terrace, Clonskeagh (now 14 Clonskeagh Road), a substantial early Victorian villa, semi-detached but not without a certain dignity, which he and Shackleton rented jointly. The main external feature is the flight of wide, shallow steps, so typical of Dublin architecture, which leads up to the front door, a stairway, it would almost seem, designed for the descent of a musical comedy Queen or, on the occasions when he was to appear in his official uniform, for an Ulster King of Arms. The staff for this modest establishment consisted of a cook, a manservant or 'boy' and a coachman.

Both men fully appreciated the somewhat muffled luxury which, in those days, could scarcely fail to mark the home of two bachelors who were, for the most part, careless of expense.

Certainly this house must have provided new standards of comfort and good taste to Sir Arthur Vicars' personal secretary, Mr Horlock, when he arrived to begin work in Dublin. Vicars kindly allowed him to stay at his house until he had found lodgings. Immediately prior to his appointment Horlock had been living at No. 13 Railway Approach, Lower Edmonton;

and it is difficult to understand why Vicars, wishing to find a
personal secretary, should have decided to advertise for one in
a London newspaper. This, however, is what happened; and it
is reassuring to know that Mr Horlock, of whom so little is
known, had been 'awarded a high character from his clergy'.

The last of Vicars' supporters on official occasions was
Francis Bennett-Goldney. He first met Vicars early in 1905,
probably at a meeting of the Society of Antiquaries, of which
both were Fellows; although, where Vicars specialised in old
books, silver and objects of heraldic interest, Goldney's tastes
were at once more catholic and less discriminating. He had already, in the face of bitter opposition, been elected Mayor of
Canterbury; and he felt an immediate interest when, shortly
after their first meeting, he learnt that Vicars might be able to
find a place for him in the Office of Arms as a junior pursuivant.

The appointment of the two heralds took place in September
1905, and it was in the following November that Goldney told
Vicars that he would like to obtain a post in the Office of Arms.
Probably Goldney's habitual directness frightened poor Ulster.
Vicars explained that, since he knew him only slightly, he would
prefer Goldney's application to be made in the form of a recom-
mendation from 'some friend of influence'. In consequence, the
Duke of Bedford[1] wrote to Lord Dudley[2] on Goldney's behalf
and, after consulting Vicars, the Lord-Lieutenant recommended
that the appointment should be made. Before this was done,
however, the Government fell and Lord Dudley was succeeded
by Lord Aberdeen. In January, 1906, the junior appointment
of Athlone Pursuivant became vacant by the resignation of
Mr H. Claude Blake; and Vicars suggested that Lord Dudley's
nomination should now be carried out. Lord Aberdeen con-
curred; but there was further delay and it was not until May,
1907, a year after Ulster had been knighted by King Edward,
that Goldney became Athlone Pursuivant.

Humbler members of the official staff were Miss Gibbon the
typist, and William Stivey the messenger, a former naval rating

---

[1] Herbrand, 11th Duke of Bedford (1858-1940).
[2] William, 2nd Earl of Dudley, Lord Lieutenant of Ireland, 1902-5.

with a small pension. Last, but by no means least, there was Mrs Mary Farrell, a hard-working widow woman who cleaned the Office of Arms and brought up her three sons in the fear of God and their own mother. Tall, slim and handsome even in her middle age, wearing with regal dignity the long velvet cloak with which, when going through the streets, she covered her working clothes, her swathed bonnet with its jet ornaments nodding and glittering in the sunlight, Mrs Farrell was, above all, a woman of character. Through the good offices of Arthur Vicars, Mrs Farrell's eldest son, Séamus,[1] had been placed on the pay-roll of the Board of Works. His tasks included shaking the mats, carrying in the dustbin and, in the winter, filling the coal-scuttles and bringing them to the doors of their respective rooms. Mrs Farrell did not allow him to enter any of the rooms 'for fear of dirtying the place'.

Vicars, contemplating the staff he had gathered round him, found good reasons for congratulating himself on his perspicacity and good fortune. He would have been much surprised if anyone had told him that the members of his court regarded each other with far less esteem than he imagined. Outwardly, however, the wheels turned smoothly enough at the Office of Arms; and there was no doubt that Vicars and his heraldic supporters provided a handsome and colourful addition to many official occasions.

2

In 1810 John Gamble, an army surgeon, wrote:[2]

> Though Dublin Castle is pretty, and even magnificent in some of its parts, it is deficient as a whole: it has no uniformity of plan, and as it is so scattered that the eye can take little of it in at once, it has no dignity of appearance – it bears too evident marks of the various repairs it has undergone . . . and has lost all traces of its venerable origin in the grotesque embellishments of modern art.

[1] Séamus O'Farrell, one of the two patriots chosen by the Countess Markievicz to post upon Dublin's walls 'the call to arms' before the Easter Rising in 1916, was later to become editor of the *Leinster Leader* and a senator in the first Dáil.

[2] J. Gamble, *Sketches of History, Politics and Manners taken in Dublin in the Autumn of 1810.*

Ninety years later this same work of transmogrification, this policy of mending and making do, was still in progress at Dublin Castle (as, in fact, it continues till this day).

Soon after the accession of Edward VII, it was decided that the Office of Arms should be transferred from the Bermingham Tower to the Bedford Tower in Upper Castle Yard, immediately opposite the Viceregal Apartments.

Vicars was delighted. With his informed taste he could scarcely fail to appreciate the charm and symmetry of his new office; and he much hoped that, in the course of the ensuing changes, he might be able to solve two problems which, occasionally, weighed upon his mind. The first of these concerned the insignia of the Order of St Patrick. When the Statutes of the Order had been revised in the time of William IV, the Jewels had been made the responsibility of the Lord-Lieutenant; but, when Vicars was created Ulster King of Arms, he found to his surprise that the regalia was to be placed in his care. During Sir Bernard Burke's reign the insignia had been kept by Messrs West and Son, the Dublin jewellers. Only when needed for some state occasion were the Jewels brought to the Castle and there, except when being actually worn by the Lord-Lieutenant, they were kept in a wall safe[1] in Burke's office in the Bermingham Tower. Vicars protested to the then Lord-Lieutenant, Lord Houghton,[2] at this unlooked for responsibility, but could not persuade him to accept their charge. Again, when Lord Houghton was succeeded by Lord Cadogan,[3] Vicars renewed his efforts to dispense with this burden but failed to secure any satisfaction.

When the move to the Bedford Tower was under discussion, Vicars again approached Lord Cadogan. He pointed out that his office was the only one in the Castle to contain objects of great intrinsic value; and he suggested that the upper part of the Bedford Tower might be converted into a flat for himself where the insignia could be safely housed. (He also hoped that in this way he might secure free accommodation for himself.) Lord Cadogan was willing to support this proposal but, before

---

[1] Still to be seen in the office of the Deputy Keeper of State Papers.

[2] Robert, Lord Houghton, Lord-Lieutenant of Ireland, 1892–5; created Marquess of Crewe, 1911.

[3] George, 5th Earl of Cadogan, Lord-Lieutenant of Ireland, 1895–1902.

it could be settled, he was replaced by Lord Dudley. Under these new circumstances Vicars was unable to persuade the Board of Works, in whose province the making of such decisions lay, that the cost of the additional alterations would be justified. In fact, the Board added a special proviso to the effect that Vicars was not to reside on the premises. The authorities agreed, however, that a strong-room should be constructed on the ground floor of the Bedford Tower to house the rare books and manuscripts belonging to the Office of Arms, as well as the regalia and other objects of value.

Plans for the strong-room were prepared by the Board of Works and approved by Vicars; but when, in 1903, the work was completed, it was found that the door was both too low and too narrow to admit the entry of the safe. Sir George Holmes, Chairman of the Board of Works, offered to take down a wall of the strong-room or, temporarily, to remove the bars from the window so that the safe might reach its appointed place. Vicars felt that the alterations had already disrupted the work of his Office for far too long, and that he himself should not be bothered with the practical details of an arrangement which Holmes and his employees, presumably experts in their own field, had bungled so badly. He declared that the safe could quite well stand in the library.

Holmes was not happy about this arrangement and neither, on more mature reflection, was Vicars. Both felt that a safe of dimensions permitting it to be carried through the door of the strong-room should be acquired; but, as Holmes pointed out, this could not be done without the sanction of the appropriate authorities. After some correspondence and at least one personal meeting, the two men reached a temporary agreement. In a minute dated 22nd December, 1903, Holmes recorded that he had had 'a conference with Ulster, who states that in view of the fact that there is always a sentry outside, the present burglar-proof safe can be used by him till such time as we can find another use for it'.

Thus it came about that the insignia and other valuables were kept in a safe in the library which was constantly used as a waiting-room by anyone calling at the Office. One door of the library was quite close to the front-door which opened into Upper Castle Yard; and a second door from the library led into the messenger's room and was ordinarily kept open; but it was subsequently established that, from his usual seat, Stivey could not see the door leading from the hall into the library. Neither could he see the safe, which stood between two of the three windows in the long wall of the library opposite to the two doors.

The revised Statutes of 1905 laid down that the insignia of the Order, together with the collars and badges of the Knights 'shall be deposited for safe-keeping in a steel safe in the Strong Room in the Chancery of the Order in the Office of Arms in Dublin'. This was a clear and unmistakable order; yet, unaccountably, Vicars ignored it entirely and left the safe, with its precious contents, in the library *cum* waiting-room. Sir George Holmes, also, who must have known the terms of the revised Statutes, does not appear to have made further efforts to find a smaller, more convenient safe.

Without the least qualm Vicars continued upon his agreeable path, here disentangling some knotty point of genealogy, there experiencing all the pleasures of the chase as he discovered and then sought to acquire some rare book, some object of *vertu*, for his collections. In fact, from 1905 until 1907, Vicars presented, had there been anyone to realise it, a spectacle less rare than is commonly appreciated: a completely happy man existing upon the very edge of a volcano.

CHAPTER TWO

1 ✄

As the date of the royal visit to Ireland and the International Exhibition drew nearer, Vicars found himself besieged with enquiries of many kinds. It must have sometimes seemed to him that the Exhibition and the royal visit had been devised solely with the intention of creating difficulties for himself.

It would not have been so bad if he had been able to delegate some of the work, as he usually could, to his nephew; but Peirce Mahony had been taken ill towards the end of April. When able to travel, he had gone down to his uncle's house at Kilmorna until, on 17th May, he crossed to England in search of a complete recovery of his health. Shackleton was engaged in his business pursuits in London, Bennett-Goldney was carrying out his mayoral duties with his usual aplomb, and Mr Burtchaell could do little more to help than supervise the day-to-day business of the Office. In addition to this unwanted influx of letters, Vicars had not only to make all the arrangements for the royal visit but he had to cope with the increasing number of people who, coming to Dublin for the Exhibition, wished for one reason or another to see him. Even during the three or four days which Goldney spent with Vicars and Shackleton in St James's Terrace for the opening of the Exhibition, he knew that Vicars had twice shown the Crown Jewels to visitors. Such incursions upon his time made even more difficult Ulster's work in connection with the impending royal visit.

That was the age of the nihilist and political assassin; and none could tell when some disgruntled enthusiast might not attempt to kill the King. This was a consideration which weighed heavily upon Lord Aberdeen and finally caused him, to the consternation of Vicars, who had just completed his programme in the belief that the King and Queen would be residing in Dublin Castle throughout their visit, to suggest to His Majesty's advisers that many inconveniences would be avoided if the royal party returned each evening to the royal yacht. To King Edward, long inured to the dangers which might at any time be directed against his august person, the suggestion that, for any reason at all, he, his Queen and the Princess Victoria should not sleep in their own royal residence while they were in Ireland, was most irritating. Finally, however, he directed the sending of a somewhat pettish telegram to say that Their Majesties and Their Household would sleep on the *Victoria and Albert*, his yacht, at Kingstown. This, coming only a few days before the arrival of the royal visitors, forced Vicars to redraft the whole of the arrangements he had already made.

It must not be imagined, however, that Vicars' time was entirely taken up with these indirect consequences of his official position. He found occasional opportunities to lay aside his preoccupation with the impending visit. We know that, between the opening of the Exhibition and the arrival of the King and Queen, he had two friends to stay with him in St James's Terrace. One of these was a Mr McEnnery, junior, of Rooskey House, Dunboyne; the other Mr Esmé Percy, at that time a very young member of Sir Frank Benson's theatrical company but later to become well-known on the British stage. Then, on 10th June, Vicars dined with his friend Mr William Chamney of Schomberg, Bray, Co. Wicklow, to meet the antiquarian Mr J. C. Hodgson, who was librarian to the Duke of Northumberland at Alnwick. They spent so agreeable an evening that it was arranged that Mr Hodgson should visit the Office of Arms upon the following day.

When he got there, Mr Hodgson would have been quite happy simply to examine the treasures on show in the strongroom and to browse among the fine collection of heraldic and genealogical books, some 1,500 in number, which Vicars had purchased with his own money and placed in the library for official and public use. He evinced little interest when Vicars offered to show him the Crown Jewels, but could scarcely refuse to look at them when they were produced from the safe. He would probably have taken more notice if he had realised that this was, so far as is known, the last time the insignia was to be seen by honest men.

Two other small details concerning Vicars' life at this time have been recorded for us. On 27th June he received a visit at the

Office of Arms from an old friend, Dr Finney of Kingston-on-Thames; and, on the following morning, when he picked up his keys from the dressing-table, he found that the latch-key which opened the front door of the Bedford Tower was missing. So, on arrival in Upper Castle Yard, he went to the police office to ask for Detective Officer Owen Kerr, one of whose duties it was to inspect the Office of Arms each evening after the staff had gone home. Kerr was out when Vicars called; but, within a very short time, he joined Ulster outside the Bedford Tower. The latter explained his predicament and asked if the detective would be so kind as to open the front door for him. Kerr was glad to do as Vicars asked, but he could not let him keep the key as he himself would be needing it that evening.

2

About eight o'clock on the morning of Wednesday, 3rd July, Mrs Farrell arrived at the Bedford Tower to carry out her daily duties with scrubbing-brush and dustpan. On that morning her son Séamus, for whom Vicars had recently found employment on the railway, had had to report for duty at 7 a.m. He had therefore delegated his duties at the Castle to his youngest brother, Patrick. This, as it turned out, was to be regretted because, when Mrs Farrell found herself faced with an entirely unprecedented situation, the older, more intelligent Séamus might have advised his mother to act more sensibly than she did.

For, when she was about to insert her key into the lock, she found that it was not necessary to do so. A mere turn of the handle opened the door, and Mrs Farrell saw that the latch of the lock was caught back.[1] This, she realised at once, could mean one of several things. Perhaps Detective Kerr had failed to secure the door when he left the Office on the previous evening; or perhaps Sir Arthur Vicars or some other member of the

---

[1] The front door of the Office of Arms, opening into the building from Upper Castle Yard, was fitted with two locks; a large stock-lock which was never used, and a latch (presumably of the Yale type) opened with a latch-key. The door was closed at night and on Sundays by slipping the snib, thus securing the door against all but the persons holding latch-keys. These people might enter the Office at any time.

staff had been working late and had left after Kerr made his duty inspection and they had, on leaving, forgotten to lock the door properly; or someone holding a key had arrived even earlier than Mrs Farrell. She had never known any of these things to happen, though she had on one occasion seen a man whom she believed to be a member of the viceregal staff let himself into the Bedford Tower shortly after she had got there.

Her obvious course would have been to notify the police of what she had found; on the other hand she had no wish to cause trouble for Sir Arthur Vicars or any other member of his staff. But she was worried by this incident. She sent Patrick home as soon as he had finished his work. Then, overcoming the rooted distrust she harboured for sailors in general and for Stivey in particular, she waited on, long after her usual time of departure, to tell the messenger, when he came on duty at ten o'clock, of what she and her son had found. This done, she left the Bedford Tower.

Vicars arrived late at the Office that morning. He was tired and out of sorts, cumbered by all he had to do in connection with the royal visit. He went up the beautiful spiral staircase which leads to the first floor and into his office. Almost at once Stivey knocked at the door and, being bidden to enter, delivered himself of the portentous news that Mrs Farrell had found the door open.

Vicars' reaction to this was altogether unexpected, out of character and remains, after more than fifty years, inexplicable.

'Did she?' he asked; or, because Stivey was afterwards not quite certain, 'Is that so?'

'Yes,' replied Stivey.

And that was all. Vicars knew he had lost his own key to the front door. The responsibility of guarding the Crown Jewels was, according to others as well as himself, a constant source of anxiety to him. Yet now, when the front door is found open, he does nothing. He neither went downstairs to try the handle of the safe, nor did he send for Detective Kerr to make sure that officer had closed the door securely when he left the Tower on the previous evening.

Yet Vicars was generally held to be over fussy about the security of the Office of Arms and its contents. . . .

CHAPTER THREE

1 ⚔

Three days later, on 6th July, came a second and even more mysterious happening. It was between seven and eight o'clock in the morning when Mrs Farrell passed the familiar scrutiny of the soldiers and police at the gates and walked towards the Bedford Tower.

Upon this day Mrs Farrell was alone, Patrick having dealt with the dustbin and the mats on the previous Wednesday. After letting herself into the hall with her latch-key she went, as was her custom, to see if any message had been left for her in Stivey's room. There were no instructions for her but, even as she crossed the threshold, she was brought up short by something she had never seen before. The door of the strong-room was partially open and, although the inner grille was locked, its key was in the lock and, depending from it by a piece of twine, was the key which opened the presses in the library.

When she had recovered from the first shock of discovery Mrs Farrell sought a measure of comfort, some time for careful thought, in following out her accustomed routine of sweeping and dusting the various rooms in preparation for the arrival of the staff.

'I was frightened,' she was to say six months later, 'and I did not know how to tell Stivey. I did not know what mark I would leave to make him see it was open, and I was going to leave a piece of paper, and then I did not because, if I left that on his table and banged the door, I thought he might think it was not open.'

For while she was cleaning the offices Mrs Farrell had decided that, as she had heard no more about her earlier discovery, her story had not been believed. This time she must leave no room for doubt.

Carefully, lest she should brush against the door of the strong-room, she removed the two keys and 'clapped' the outer

3

door. Then, putting the keys on Stivey's table, she wrote laboriously on a piece of blotting paper an explanation of what she had found and done.

'Mr Stivey,' she wrote, 'I found the strong-room door open this morning. I have closed it and I closed the gate and leave the keys on your table.'

Having written this message, she still waited for Stivey. ('I waited for a long time, for a good bit, and he did not come in.') Then, because this was a Saturday morning and she had other work to do, Mrs Farrell left the Office.

Stivey arrived as usual at ten o'clock. He found the keys, read Mrs Farrell's note and at once entered the strong-room to satisfy himself that nothing was missing. So far as he could see everything was as it should be. Then he set to his daily work[1] and waited for Vicars to come.

Stivey cannot have been in his room when Sir Arthur arrived, and it was about twelve o'clock when the messenger went up to tell his chief about Mrs Farrell's new discovery. He found, however, that Vicars was talking to Peirce Mahony, Mr Horlock and Miss Gibbon. Feeling that it would be better to speak to Vicars when he was alone, Stivey returned to his own room.

Time would seem to have been a factor, in the Dublin of 1907, of which no one took very close account. Just as Mrs Farrell could not be more precise as to her time of arrival that morning than to say that it was between seven and eight o'clock, so it was later found impossible to say when Vicars was told of Mrs Farrell's discovery except that Stivey spoke to him at some time between half past twelve and two o'clock.

As had happened on the previous Wednesday, Vicars received the news with a sang-froid which would, under many other circumstances, have been altogether admirable.

'Did she?' he asked; or 'Is that so?'

Then, without waiting for an answer, he climbed the stairs to his room.

---

[1] Stivey himself described his work as : 'Duties pretty general, from answering the door and attending the people who might call and showing them up to Sir Arthur, and things of that kind, and almost entire charge; and my room was next the strong-room door and there was an understanding that I was to allow nobody except Sir Arthur Vicars or staff, authorised persons, to pass in or out of the strong-room . . . No other duties except to take books out and put them back if ordered to do so.'

Clearly Stivey might have taken some action on his own initiative; but it has to be remembered that he had been trained in the British naval tradition of absolute obedience to one's superiors. During the six years he had been employed at the Office of Arms he had shown himself sober, conscientious and willing, virtues which had brought him to the level of pay at which he received no less than twenty-one shillings a week. While, in a perfect world, both he and Mrs Farrell might have done other than they did, neither could really be expected to take any step which might jeopardise their employment. With Vicars, however, the position was altogether different; and his role of masterly inactivity on this occasion was to be regarded by many as unpardonable.

✻

Now it was a quarter past two. In those halcyon days the Office of Arms remained open to the public on Saturdays until two o'clock, after which members of the staff would remain on to clear up any arrears of work. Stivey, however, was permitted to go home after two o'clock if he was not needed for any particular reason. Upon that afternoon, because of the approaching royal visit, many of the officials and their staff were at work but Stivey could think of nothing else that he should do. But he never departed without first obtaining Vicars' permission. He left his room and climbed the spiral stair. On the first floor he knocked at Vicars' door. The hour of doom was upon them.

2

Peirce Mahony returned to Dublin from England on the morning of 3rd July. He did not visit the Office of Arms until the 4th, but he was there on the two following days. Even though Vicars was absorbed in his work connected with the King's visit, it is odd that he never mentioned to his nephew that Mrs Farrell had found the front door of the Bedford Tower open.

On the Saturday Mahony arrived before his uncle, as it was he who received the messenger from Messrs West and Son. The man was expected, for he was bringing the gold and enamelled collar of the Order of St Patrick which had formerly been worn by the recently deceased Lord de Ros. This had been sent to the jewellers to have that peer's name inscribed on the back of one of the links in the chain. Now it was ready to be used at the investiture of Lord Castletown which was to take place while King Edward was in Dublin. Mahony accepted the parcel, removed the wrappings to make sure that the collar was in its wooden box and gave the man a receipt. Then he placed the box on his uncle's desk.

Later, as we know, he had been one of those conversing with Vicars when Stivey made his first attempt to tell the King of Arms about Mrs Farrell's new discoveries. Afterwards he had left to get some lunch but had returned and was with his uncle when Stivey knocked at the door.

As the messenger came into the room, and before he had time to ask if he might go home, Vicars rose from his seat at the desk, picked up the box containing the jewelled collar and moved round to stand between the end of his desk and the window.

'I wish you would take this collar and put it down in the safe,' he said to Stivey. 'We are getting overcrowded here; we are getting congested.'

Stivey was astounded at this request, for Vicars had never before asked him to open the safe in the library. But he took the box and waited in perplexed silence while Vicars produced a bunch of keys from his pocket and handed them to the messenger, singling out for him the one which would open the safe. Stivey left the room and went down the stairs.

Although he had never opened a safe, he was not ignorant of the procedure to be followed. Not only had he watched Vicars on many occasions but the door of the safe, with its upper and lower keyholes and its central turning lever or handle, was very similar to the larger door of the strong-room, of which he held a key.

Crossing the hall and going into the empty library, he placed the box on a table near the safe. He inserted the key into the lower keyhole, as was his practice in opening the door of the strong-room, but it would not turn. Wondering if the mechanism of the safe worked on an opposite system to that of the strong-room, he placed the key in the upper keyhole. Turning it he grasped the central handle, but it would not move. Stivey at once realised what had happened. Instead of unlocking the door he had locked it. This meant that the safe had been unlocked before he entered the room.

'It means getting somebody else,' he thought. This was a crisis beyond his experience, his abilities and his status in the office. He must report it at once. Removing the key from the door and straightening up from the crouched position he had assumed before the safe, he picked up the wooden box and turned towards the door. As he did so he heard footsteps crossing the floor above. He hurried to the foot of the staircase and, looking up, he saw Vicars about to come down. Without a word he went up to meet him.

It would appear that Vicars had scarcely given the box and keys to Stivey before he realised that he should not have delegated this task to the messenger. So, leaving his letter unfinished, he hurried from the room. When, six days later, he was questioned by the police, he told them that 'about a minute' had elapsed before he followed Stivey, whom, he said, he found at the safe.

'Stivey informed me,' he told the police, 'that the safe was unlocked, because he could not get the key into the proper slot.'

He may well be pardoned if, in view of the catastrophic discovery he was about to make, his remembrance of those intervening moments was at fault. Stivey's account does seem the more probable and circumstantial. According to the messenger he said to Vicars, when they met on the staircase.

'Sir Arthur, the last time you were at the safe, you could not have locked the door.'

'Oh,' said Vicars, 'I must have done.'

'Well, Sir Arthur, I find that the safe door is unlocked.'

'Oh, you didn't. What do you mean?'

'So,' continued the messenger, 'Sir Arthur came down with me and came over here,[1] and then I was able to show Sir Arthur Vicars the exact state in which I found the lock when I came to it. Sir Arthur himself opened the safe door, and the first thing Sir Arthur Vicars said on opening the safe door was:

---

[1] The Commission of Inquiry, before which Stivey gave evidence, met in the library of the Office of Arms.

' "The key is in the lock. I wonder if they are all right,"
meaning, I suppose, the Crown Jewels. With that Sir Arthur
opened that case and then he opened this, and went down on
one knee and said:

' "My God, they are gone," he said, "The Jewels are gone!" '

The first case Vicars opened was that which should have contained the Crown Jewels. Then he opened another, a box similar
to that which Stivey had carried down, and, as he did so, he
exclaimed, 'Lord Cork's collar gone! Anything else?' In des-
peration he began a systematic search of the wooden boxes
which had contained the Knights' collars and, as each was
revealed to be empty save for the tissue paper in which the
chains had been wrapped, he exclaimed over and over again in
a litany of suffering, 'This gone!' and 'This gone!'

A jewel case containing the Mahony family diamonds had
disappeared altogether, taken no doubt because, whereas the
keys of the other boxes were kept in the safe, Vicars' stepbrother, Mr George Mahony, had retained the keys of this
himself.

When Vicars had opened all the boxes, there remained in the
safe only three objects, the wills drawn up by George Mahony
and Arthur Vicars, and the patent creating the latter Ulster King
of Arms. For all its fine engrossing, its royal seal and signature,
this document was now no more than a mockery and a reproach
to the guardian who had failed so signally to guard the Order's
insignia.

Vicars realised, just as Stivey had, that this was a situation
with which he could not deal himself. He told the messenger to
go to the Commissioners of Police and ask one of them to come
to him at once and, after he had done that, to inform the
Detective Department of what had happened.

Only when Stivey had left him did Vicars call up the stairs to
his nephew. Peirce Mahony came down to find his uncle 'looking ghastly white', the empty morocco case open in his hand.

'Gone!' exclaimed Vicars as Mahony came into the room.

When the young man was asked what was said after that, he
could not remember. Nor was he able to throw any further light
upon the exact sequence of events after his uncle had given the
box and the keys to Stivey. He explained his unawareness by
saying that he had only just returned from lunch.

Then came a curious hiatus. Stivey had no distance to go to reach the police office; but it was not until after three o'clock, probably rather later, that the Assistant Commissioner of the Dublin Metropolitan Police, Mr W.V.Harrel, M.V.O., was told of what had happened.

Meanwhile Vicars remained with his nephew beside the empty safe; but it was half-past three before either of them remembered that Mr Burtchaell was still on the premises and must be told.

If we are to credit the charges levelled against Burtchaell by T.M.Healy, Vicars' right-hand man may well have welcomed his chief's extraordinary news as serving to distract his thoughts from his own troubles. For, according to Healy, it had been on the previous day, 5th July, that Burtchaell had sworn an affidavit knowing the information contained therein to be false.[1]

'I was in my own room,' Burtchaell was to testify later, 'I was just preparing to go away when he [Vicars] came in and told me that a dreadful thing had happened. I thought . . . it was something that had happened to the King about his visit to this country, and then he told me that the safe had been opened and that the collars and Jewels had been all taken out and taken away. I said it was a dreadful thing, and he told me to say nothing about it.'

Burtchaell, ever the practical man of affairs, now attempted to take charge of the situation. He asked if the police had been informed. When told that Stivey had gone to do this, he persuaded Vicars to try and establish when the safe had last been opened and the Jewels known to have been safely inside. Because of the large number of visitors to the Office in recent weeks this was not as easy to settle as it would have been ordinarily; but, in the end, Vicars decided that he had shown the insignia either to Mr Hodgson on 10th June or to Dr Finney on 27th June. Vicars, in his shocked condition, could not remember which. Burtchaell then said that Vicars must telegraph at once to both these gentlemen to ask whether or not they had seen the Jewels. He thought that to have this point settled might be of material assistance to the police.

---

[1] See T. M. Healy's *Stolen Waters* (1913), p. 455 *et seq.* and *The Great Fraud of Ulster* (1917), p. 164 *et seq.*, for details of Lord Shaftesbury's claim to the waters of Lough Neagh, a claim chiefly established on Burtchaell's evidence.

Vicars, however, demurred, displaying an almost childish
obstinacy in his desire to prevent, or at least to delay, any hint
of the loss becoming public. Burtchaell pointed out the folly of
this attitude. There could be no possible harm in telegraphing to
ask if the two men had seen the Jewels. In the end Vicars agreed
to tell the police that, to the best of his remembrance, either Mr
Hodgson or Dr Finney had been the last person to whom he had
shown the insignia.

Surprisingly, it was not until this had been decided that they
came downstairs. One would have expected that anyone, told of
the robbery, would have gone at once to the library. Mother
Hubbard's dog almost certainly attempted to investigate the
cupboard to make sure that his mistress was not mistaken.

After they had joined Mahony in the library, Burtchaell
asked when the theft had been discovered and, not quite truth-
fully perhaps, Vicars said it was very shortly before Burtchaell
himself had been told. He then went on to say that 'burglars had
broken into the office', and, a little later, that 'he was at the
strong-room also'.

Burtchaell waited for some amplification of this statement.
He thought Vicars must have discovered signs of an attempt to
enter the strong-room; but Vicars said nothing more. Realising
the great shock all this had been to his chief, Burtchaell refrained from asking further questions. In the uneasy silence
which followed, while they waited for the curiously delayed
appearance of the police, the three men stood in front of the
open, empty safe, each of them busy with his own unspoken
thoughts.

3

Superintendent John Lowe of the Detective Branch of the
Dublin Metropolitan Police was the first police official to arrive
at the scene of the crime. Once again there is this odd lack of
clock consciousness among the Irish, for the Superintendent
could not be more precise than to say he reached the office between three and four o'clock.

Stivey brought Lowe into the library, where they found
Vicars and his companions beside the safe. Now the shadowy,

enigmatic figure of Mr Horlock had joined the bewildered little group which, had an artist chosen to depict its members in this immediate aftermath of crisis, could not have been described as a conversation-piece. All were waiting for someone to come and take command, someone who would act with the initiative and authority which, it was all too clear, were beyond poor Vicars' grasp. He raised his head as Lowe entered the room.

'A burglary has been committed here,' he said, 'right under our noses.'

The Superintendent asked what had been taken.

'The Jewels have been stolen from this safe,' Vicars explained. 'In fact a clean sweep has been made of the safe.'

As he showed Lowe the empty cases, he told how he had asked Stivey to put away the gold collar for him and of how the messenger had found the safe unlocked.

In the red morocco case which had held the Crown Jewels, Lowe noticed a small piece of blue ribbon. This, Vicars told him, had been attached to the badge of the Order by a clasp fastened with two small screws and run on to a hook on the badge. It would be difficult, he said, to detach the ribbon from the badge as the screws were very fine and, in consequence, difficult to manipulate. Even when the screws had been removed, it would require some delicate coaxing to take the ribbon from the hook without damaging it. Vicars estimated that the whole operation could not be done in less then ten minutes. No one could think of any reason why such care should have been taken with this scrap of material. No one ever put forward any valid explanation for this. It did, however, suggest to Lowe that the silk had been removed by someone accustomed to handle the Jewels and familiar with the mechanism of those delicate screws. But his suggestion that the larceny had been an 'inside job' was met by Vicars with a vigorous denial. He refused to accept even the possibility that anyone on the staff could be guilty of the theft.

Not long after Lowe had begun his investigation, Mr Harrel arrived.

'The Crown Jewels are gone,' Vicars told him as he came into the library. Then, after repeating his account of how the loss was discovered, he continued, 'This is the fault of the Board of Works. I asked them for a safe in the strong-room and they did not give it. If they had given it, this would not have happened.'

'Did you actually ask for a safe in the strong-room?' asked Harrel.

'Yes,' replied Vicars. 'I have the correspondence.'

Harrel, once he had grasped the essential facts so far as they were then understood, wished to know when the Jewels were last seen, and was told what Vicars had said on this point. He showed no sympathy for Ulster's hesitancy to get in touch with his two friends, and told him bluntly that he must telegraph at once to Dr Finney and Mr Hodgson. Vicars again demurred and then became very excited. After Burtchaell had joined his arguments with those of the Assistant Commissioner, Vicars finally agreed to do as they advised. He sat down to compose a telegram, but it was soon evident that even this was beyond his powers. Realising this, Harrel dictated what he should write.

AM ANXIOUS TO KNOW LATEST DATE ON WHICH SAFE WITH JEWELS WAS OPENED. DO YOU RECOLLECT WHETHER I SHOWED THEM TO YOU WHEN HERE ON 10TH [27TH] JUNE. WIRE REPLY, LETTER FOLLOWS, VICARS, CASTLE.[1]

Soon replies to both telegrams were received. Dr Finney said he had not seen the jewels, while Mr Hodgson declared that he had, but not on the date mentioned. It had been on 11th June that he had visited the Office of Arms. Thus it was established that the jewels were safe on that date.

❦

It was about a quarter past four when Detective Officer Owen Kerr first heard that something was wrong at the office. Going there at once, he found the whole party in the library. Stivey went into the hall when he heard Kerr unlocking the door, but the detective could not afterwards remember whether Stivey had returned to the library with him. Ulster turned to the detective with an entirely new suggestion.

'Kerr,' he said, 'the Jewels are all gone. Some of the smart boys that have been over for the King's visit have made a clean sweep of them.'

---

[1] The telegrams and letters sent to Mr Hodgson were given by him to Mr Chamney and are now preserved in the Genealogical Office, Dublin.

Kerr paid little attention to this. He asked how it came about that the safe was open.

'The Board of Works again,' Vicars told him. 'I have asked them for a good safe, for which I have correspondence to show, and they refused it and they did not give it to me. I have no confidence in this safe.' Then, after once more telling how the loss was discovered, he said, 'I sent Stivey with a collar, and he came and found it open.'

'Though I am here a little over six years,' put in Stivey, 'I never had the key in my hand before.'

'Yes, that is so,' said Vicars. 'I was thronged owing to pressure of business and I sent Stivey, but I was coming immediately after him. That key was always in my possession and I never let it out of it before.'

Vicars believed this when he said it, but later inquiries were to show that once, when the Office of Arms was still situated in the Bermingham Tower, he had asked Burtchaell to open the safe for him.

Shortly after Kerr's arrival, someone – he could not afterwards remember who it was – asked Vicars whether the diamonds could be identified. He replied that they could. The jewellers had told him that, should the insignia be lost or stolen it would be possible to identify the stones even if they were removed from their settings.

'What about the strong-room?' asked Superintendent Lowe. 'Were there any marks on the door or anything missing from it?'

'No, it's a Milner's safe,' Vicars told him, 'and it is quite secure. Milner or Chubb locks are burglar-proof.'

After some more conversation which the police evidently did not think worth recording, Vicars returned to the subject of the strong-room.

'It's burglar-proof,' he remarked, 'and could not be opened, only by its own key.'

Nothing was said about the door of the strong-room having been found open that morning. Nor does it appear that Stivey realised that Vicars was not being entirely frank with the police. He had to admit the various visitors to the Office when they rang the bell. He also saw most of them to the door when they left; and no one, afterwards, could be quite certain what portions of Vicars' statement Stivey had or had not heard.

The last visitor to the Bedford Tower that afternoon was Sir John Ross of Bladensburg, Chief Commissioner of the Dublin Metropolitan Police. Once more the story was told; but he was chiefly struck by the scrap of blue ribbon and anxious to discover why it had been left behind.

'I suppose it is cut?' he asked and, when Vicars told him that it had not been, he observed that the thief was plainly not concerned about the length of time he spent over the abstraction of the Jewels. Not only had the ribbon been removed from the Badge with great care, but the tissue paper wrappings had all been neatly folded and replaced in the wooden boxes. It was all very different to the methods employed by most burglars, who are anxious only to secure their loot and, as quickly as possible, to leave the scene of the crime. They rarely tidy up.

The Superintendent now set himself to discover who held keys to the various doors; and, although he interrogated Vicars on this point, other police were to return to the subject again and again until the facts were clearly established.

To the front door of the Office there were seven keys. Six of these were held by Vicars, Burtchaell, Mahony,[1] Stivey, Kerr and Mrs Farrell. The seventh was in the possession of John O'Keefe, whose duty it was during the Dublin Season to climb nightly to the lantern above the Bedford Tower and light the lamp which, later, he must needs extinguish. O'Keefe was able to satisfy the police that he had not entered the Office of Arms since the Season ended about 24th March.

There were only two keys to the safe, both retained by Vicars. One he carried usually on a ring with other keys; the other was hidden under some old papers in a cupboard forming the lower part of a bookcase at his house in St James's Terrace. He was certain that only he knew where this second key was kept.

At first the police took little interest in the keys of the strong-room, since they had not yet learnt that the door had been found open; but they later ascertained that there were four keys to the

---

[1] Before he left for England, Mahony had placed his keys in a locked desk in his house, the key of the desk remaining always on his watch-chain.

outer door. Vicars, Mahony and Stivey each held one. The fourth, previously carried by Burtchaell, had been handed back to Vicars about a year before. This had been wrapped in a piece of oiled paper and placed in an unlocked drawer in a chest in the strong-room. Vicars believed that only he and Stivey knew where this key had been secreted.

To the inner door of the strong-room, the iron grille, there were two keys. One was kept upstairs, presumably in Vicars' office. The other (to which the key of the library presses was attached) remained in the lock except when Stivey had to leave his room for any reason. On those occasions he removed the key from the lock and placed both keys in the drawer of his table, so that any member of the staff, wishing to enter the strong-room or to obtain a book from the library, could do so without delay.

This interrogation of Vicars went on for two and a half hours; but, although they felt increasingly certain that the theft had been carried out by someone connected with the Office of Arms, and though they knew that Vicars was the only person authorised to hold keys opening the front door, the safe and the strong-room, none of the detectives believed that he had played a voluntary part in the theft of the Jewels.

4

When at last permitted to go to his own room, Vicars at once sat down to write to Dr Finney and Mr Hodgson. He also wished to send two further telegrams.

To Mr Hodgson he wrote:

> Many thanks for your prompt reply to my wire. A dreadful thing has happened. On going to the safe in my Office today to lock up the late Lord de Ros's Collar, which had just been returned to me, to my horror I found the contents of the safe had been rifled & the Crown Jewels removed from their case & 5 Gold Collars of the Order of St Patrick (valued at £280 a piece) removed from their cases, & alas! my brother's jewel box in which were my mother's diamonds gone, which he had asked me to keep for him in

safe custody. In fact the only things left were the empty cases & their two wills!

I wanted to tell the Police the last time I knew the contents were safe – and the only 2 people I could remember lately being in the Office to whom I might have shown them, & I thought I had to one or the other, was yourself & Dr Finney of Kingston-on-Thames – he is an old friend of mine. I therefore wired to you and him. He was at Office on 26th June & you on the 10th Monday. He replied 'No, that he had not been shown them.' So it takes us back nearly a month when I knew all was safe.

You say in your wire Tuesday the 11th but I think you must be mistaken as we met at Chamney's on the Saturday & you came in on Monday 10th. It is not of much importance only a day.

It is awful for me, but what more can mortal do when a safe is picked as appears to be the case, for no sign of tampering with safe or lock is visible.

The Police are hard at it & the hue & cry will be raised all over Europe but for the present, please, keep this to yourself.

I must end to catch post. Any details you can remember will be valued, such as whether you recollect my putting all away & locking safe. It was found unlocked – but I can swear I locked it.

Yours sincerely, A. Vicars, Ulr.

It was probably while he was writing this and a similar letter to Dr Finney that Vicars was interrupted by the arrival of Mr Harrel. The Assistant Commissioner had returned to his office some time earlier, leaving Superintendent Lowe to obtain accurate descriptions of the missing jewels and collars. Now he wished to ask further questions about the keys.

Vicars was not at all pleased. He felt there had already been far too many questions and insufficient action. Besides, he was anxious to finish his letters. So, intending to make his own position regarding the keys perfectly clear, he launched into a description of the great care he had always taken of the keys to the safe. The one he used, he said, was always on his key-ring and never left his possession.

Harrel, however, was not easy to persuade.

'Now, is that really the case?' he asked. 'It is not a thing that many people could say.'

'Yes,' Vicars assured him. 'They have never left my possession. I have always been most careful.'

'For instance,' Harrel began to probe more deeply, 'on the occasion of a function at the Castle, when you are here in uniform, how do you carry that bunch of keys in your uniform?'

'Oh well, on a night of that sort, of course, I put the keys in my overcoat pocket.'

Quick as the proverbial flash, Harrel seized upon this exception to the golden rule.

'And what do you do with the overcoat?'

'I leave it in Herschell's[1] room.'

(In a subsequent statement Vicars explained that he had a special pocket made in his uniform for the safe key, which he removed from the bunch of other keys before leaving these in his overcoat pocket.)

Harrel then asked him about the second key to the safe. Would he be good enough to go back at once to St James's Terrace to make sure that it was still in its hiding-place? Vicars was by this time in no mood to be ordered about in his own office. He told the Assistant Commissioner that he was too busy to go just then. He would leave about seven o' clock and would telephone to Harrel as soon as he had made sure that the second key was safe. And with this the Assistant Commissioner had to be content; but, almost as though to make amends for his refusal, Vicars suddenly produced an entirely new suspect for Harrel's consideration. He suggested that Arthur Phillips, his coachman, might be responsible for the theft.

Phillips, a married man with four children, had been in Vicars' service for the past seven years; but at this time he was under notice to leave, for what reason is not stated. Nor do we know what prompted Vicars to make this accusation against him, except that, about eleven months earlier, Phillips had been for a short time in possession of the keys.

For the police soon realised that, despite his protestations to the contrary, Vicars had not always retained the keys in his

---

[1] Richard Farrer, 2nd Baron Herschell (1879-1929), Private Secretary to the Lord-Lieutenant of Ireland, 1905-7.

keeping. Only two months before, he had left his keys, including that of the safe, in his writing-table at St James's Terrace.
Elizabeth Darcy, his housekeeper, had found them and sent the
footman, Frederick Pitt, to the Castle with them. Vicars, in
admitting this lapse, said the keys were not out of his possession
for more than an hour.

As neither Mrs Darcy nor Pitt was ever suspected of having
anything to do with the theft, it is clear that there must have
been special circumstances to make Vicars accuse Phillips. We
are, however, given no clue as to their nature. The police were
soon able to satisfy themselves that Phillips was innocent and,
within a short time, Vicars himself abandoned his suspicions.

That miserable Saturday dragged slowly on, with the police no
nearer the discovery of any clue. At last, probably a little before
seven o'clock, Vicars left the Office of Arms and went to St
James's Terrace. Not for him, on that evening, the comfort of
the Kildare Street Club at which he so often called before going
home to dine. On reaching his house, he went at once to the cupboard in which he had secreted the second key to the safe. Then
he telephoned to Harrel, telling him the key was safe and did not
appear to have been disturbed.

A lonely dinner can have brought him but small measure of
comfort; but, when Peirce Mahony called shortly afterwards, he
found his uncle much more composed and able to deal with
practical details than he had been when at the Castle. Mahony
had not come entirely on a visit of sympathy. It is difficult to
understand why, now that almost everything of value had been
removed from the Office of Arms, he should have been so anxious to get rid of his keys; but that was his purpose in coming to
Clonskeagh. He gave to Vicars his keys to the front door and the
strong-room.

After Mahony left, Vicars wrote again to Mr Hodgson. The
latter's quibble about the date of his visit must have worried
Vicars, who had now cleared up the matter satisfactorily.

Since writing in a hurry to catch post, I have looked up
my own diary & find that you are quite right in saying you

called at the Office on Tuesday 11th June for I find I dined with Chamney on the 10th, but my Office Messenger had got your name down in the call book at the Office on Monday.

The object in view is to fix a date for the Police when I can state absolutely that all was secure.

The safe is a fine one (Radcliffe and Horner) & the key of it never left my possession. It was always a source of anxiety to me, having charge of things of such value &, during the Castle Season, I had to take them to the Lord Lieutenant on full-dress nights and again get them up & lock them in the safe, often at 3 a.m. But the Police were always about & a Detective patrolled thro' my Office at night. The safe, as you know, was just inside a window outside which a sentry patrolled night and day & the Guard Room of Castle was next my Office!!

The lock must have been picked or else a duplicate key got. The safe was supplied in 1893 by the Board of Works. What greater precautions could I have taken? I have had to write to my brother to tell him of our mother's diamonds having been taken, in fact they made a clean sweep of St Patrick, collars & all. My only hope is that the stones may be traced as they were of the very finest Brazilian stones of the finest water & such as can't be had now at any price & would be sure to be spotted in the diamond market if they appeared.

You can imagine how I feel, these things taken almost from under one's nose in a Royal Palace, 2 or 3 yards from the Guard.

Please keep these details as private as I understand the Police wish it for the present.

I am much obliged for your prompt reply to my wire.

Yours sincerely, A. Vicars, Ulr.

It is clear from this that Vicars was by no means convinced that Phillips was the culprit. This letter also provides an indication of the way in which Vicars would groom facts to fit in with what he felt the public should be told. Kerr's nightly inspection of the Bedford Tower could not possibly, with any degree of truth, be described as a patrol, a word which suggests

4

that a detective moved restlessly from room to room throughout the night. As for the way in which Stivey kept the Visitors' Book, it was found that there was a similar doubt as to whether Dr Finney had called at the Office on 26th or 27th June.

Also during that evening Vicars despatched two telegrams; one to Bennett-Goldney, asking him to expedite his travelling arrangements so that he would arrive in Dublin on the Monday instead of on the Tuesday. The other was to Shackleton, asking him to take to Scotland Yard a copy of the printed Statutes of the Order of St Patrick. The police needed this in order to draw up accurate descriptions of the missing Jewels and collars.

Although it is unlikely that Goldney received his telegram until the Sunday morning, he at once made arrangements to catch the Irish mail that evening.

5

Since he was a devout and enthusiastic adherent of the Established Church of Ireland, spending much time and ingenuity upon the beautifying of the more 'advanced' Protestant churches in and around Dublin, it is unlikely that Vicars stayed away from church that Sunday morning. Apart, however, from that, he remained at home working with Mr Horlock on the final details connected with the royal visit. Whatever may have been his shortcomings, he possessed the ability to become wholly absorbed in his work; and even then, less than twenty-four hours after the discovery of the theft, he was able to forget the anxieties which had plagued him throughout the night.

'It was not,' he told the police a few days later, 'until Sunday afternoon . . . that I realised that the strong-room door was open on Saturday morning. I said to Horlock that I must ask Stivey this point in the morning.'

By the morning, however, it was not Vicars but the police who would be questioning the messenger.

Throughout the Saturday night and Sunday morning the detectives continued their investigations. Not until three o'clock on the Sunday afternoon, a time not customarily regarded as conducive to anything but sleep and sleep's related pleasures, did the police receive any light on the mystery.

Because they had been told that Mrs Farrell usually left the Office of Arms before the staff arrived in the mornings, none of the police had expected that she might give them any material assistance. Nevertheless, as a matter of routine investigation, Kerr called at the house where Mrs Farrell lived with her three sons. In the course of the conversation he had with her, he realised that his superiors would have to re-shape drastically any theories they might have formed so far.

Never suspecting that nothing had been said to the authorities about the doors she had found unlocked, Mrs Farrell told Kerr how, both on the Wednesday and the Saturday, she had reported her discoveries to Stivey. Despite his anxiety to report these facts to his superiors, Kerr waited until he had obtained a clear picture of Mrs Farrell's astonishing story. He also collected, either on this occasion or during some subsequent interview within the next few days, an odd story that was to cause more than a little alarm and despondency in viceregal circles.

It appeared that, some five or six months earlier, Mrs Farrell had been about her accustomed duties on the first floor of the Bedford Tower when she heard someone moving about downstairs. Going out on to the landing, she saw a gentleman cross the hall beneath her. As he opened the door of the library he looked up and saw her. 'It's all right,' (he told her reassuringly) or something like that.

When called upon to give evidence regarding this incident some six months later, Mrs Farrell continued:

'I looked at him and the sun was in my sight, and he, like, stopped there at the end of that desk and I did not like it. I did not know whether he was a gentleman connected with the office or not, and he apparently came down to this end as if to write a note, and he then went out again, and he nodded to me and I thought he was some gentleman connected with the office, and then I came to see if there was a note on that table and there was no note. All this happened about ten in the morning before Stivey came in'.

Asked by the Solicitor-General whether she saw what this strange visitor was doing in the library, Mrs Farrell replied:

'No, I did not. I was always very anxious. I listened on the stairs and I did not like to go on with my work, and I did not like to ask questions, but he came down to that table.'

But when Kerr had first heard this story and had asked Mrs Farrell if she had recognised the gentleman in the library, she replied without hesitation that it had been Lord Haddo, the eldest son of the Lord-Lieutenant. Either then or after he had discussed this story with his superiors, Kerr attempted to throw doubts upon her identification. He asked Mrs Farrell whether she had ever been close to Lord Haddo. Had she ever spoken to him? When she gave a negative reply to both these questions, he pointed out to her how easy it would be for a clever lawyer to cast doubts upon her story and to make her look ridiculous. After all, she had said that the sun was in her eyes. Could she seriously consider going into a witness-box and declaring that it was Lord Haddo whom she had seen in the library that morning some months earlier?

The threat of ridicule is a powerful weapon in the hands of the police when they are questioning a decent kindly woman who wishes to do nothing to undermine the authority she must, if she is to do her duty, continue to exercise over her three sons. It is not surprising that Mrs Farrell decided that, if the police were not interested in accepting her identification of that early morning visitor, she would not press it on them. Nevertheless Mrs Farrell remained convinced that it was Lord Haddo she had seen; and her sons, all of them tenuously connected with the Office of Arms and so, inevitably, much questioned by their friends and acquaintances about the theft, felt no doubt that their mother was in this, as in every other department of life, infallible. Thus, we are convinced, it was through the crass stupidity of the authorities in refusing to sift the truth or false-hood of Mrs Farrell's story that there grew a crop of rumours and conjecture which must have been extremely painful to the already harassed Aberdeens and to Lord and Lady Haddo.

On that Sunday afternoon, however, Kerr was primarily anxious to let his superiors know all he had learnt from Mrs Farrell about the doors she had found open. Inexplicably, no attempt was made that day to question either Vicars or Stivey.

6

On Monday 8th July, Francis Bennett-Goldney, Athlone Pursuivant, walked down the gangway of the mail-boat into the vert and argent of a fine Dublin morning. Despite an unexpectedly rough crossing, he had been buoyed up through the uneasy tedium of his journey by the thought that, within a very few days, he would be taking part in the splendid ceremony of the installation of a Knight Companion of the Order of St Patrick, himself in personal attendance upon his Sovereign.

Arriving at the house in St James's Terrace, he was informed that Vicars was still in bed. The latter was, however, wide awake and, despite his usual sanguine outlook, looked profoundly distressed.

'Have you heard the awful news?' he asked as Goldney entered his room.

His guest replied that he had heard nothing, whereupon Vicars told him of the horror which had overwhelmed him.

'I cannot give you the details of the conversation,' Goldney was to say six months later. 'It ended in my going to my own room and having a bath. . . . I was feeling very tired and had a bath and rested, and had some breakfast then.'

Nevertheless, despite his fatigue and the disagreeable effects of the crossing, Vicars' news did much to restore Goldney's customary interest in the world around him. While waiting without much enthusiasm for breakfast, he felt sufficiently recovered to write one or two letters. Not often can so luscious a plum of gossip have dropped into Mr Bennett-Goldney's lap. He must make immediate use of it.

※

Meanwhile the police had renewed their questioning of William Stivey. Why had he told them nothing of the doors which Mrs Farrell had found open?

The messenger sought refuge in an injured innocence. Had he not done everything a man could be expected to do? Had he not told Sir Arthur Vicars, both on the Wednesday and the Saturday, of what Mrs Farrell said she had found?

So he had told Sir Arthur? And if he had, what action had

Ulster taken? So far as Stivey knew, he had done nothing. This the police could not believe; but nothing they could say made Stivey alter his story in any way. So they turned to another question. Why, since Stivey had listened to Ulster making his statement to the police in the library, had he not drawn their attention to the fact that nothing had been said regarding Mrs Farrell's discoveries?

Stivey told him that, although it was true that he was in the library when Sir Arthur Vicars and the other members of the staff were being interrogated, he had had, on a number of occasions, to admit police officers and others who had been summoned to the Office of Arms, as well as seeing to the door those who wished to leave the building. Because of these interruptions he had not realised that Ulster had said nothing of Mrs Farrell's discoveries.

The police, unable to make any progress in this direction, now asked the messenger when he had left the Office on the previous Tuesday evening. Had it been before or after Sir Arthur Vicars went home?

Stivey could not be certain. Of one thing, however, he was sure. When leaving the building he had, as usual, slipped down the snib of the lock before he closed the door behind him. No one, from the outside, could have opened the front door without using a key. Only one piece of information, probably irrelevant, emerged during this exchange. It appeared that, whereas before Horlock's coming it had been Vicars' habit to leave the Office at the same time as Stivey, he now stayed on later with his personal secretary in the otherwise deserted building.

When he was asked about the sequence of events on the evening of the previous Friday, Stivey had no difficulty in giving a very clear account of what had happened immediately before he left the Office. It had been between half-past five and a quarter to six when he went up to ask Ulster if he might go home. Being told that he might, he had asked if Sir Arthur would be wishing to go into the strong-room again that evening. Vicars then picked up a manuscript he had had to consult that day and handed it to Stivey, asking him to replace it in the strong-room. Stivey had taken the manuscript and gone downstairs. Apart from the fact that he was often asked to return books and manuscripts to their places in the library and strong-room, this incident provides a curious foreshadowing of what was to take place on the following day when Vicars handed the wooden box to the messenger.

On the Friday evening, however, Stivey had found nothing to disturb his peace of mind. The glass case within the strong-room, its front secured by four locks, had presented to the messenger's gaze its familiar and splendid display. For here, despite the injunctions contained in the Statutes of the Order, were kept no less than three collars and badges belonging to Knights of St Patrick, as well as two silver maces, the Irish Sword of State, a jewelled sceptre, two massive silver spurs and the gilt crown which, with a gold and enamelled badge and gilt collar, were worn on ceremonial occasions by Vicars as Ulster King of Arms. Elsewhere in the strong-room, in a drawer, were yet another collar and badge; but these, of course, Stivey did not see as he glanced round the room before closing the grille behind him. He left in the lock its key, from which hung that opening the presses in the library. He had closed the outer door of the strong room, making sure that it was securely locked. Then, satisfied that all was well, he left the building.

At this point the police dismissed Stivey and began to review the new material they had gathered. Detective Officer Kerr was able to supplement this. He was certain that, on the Tuesday evening, the front door had been locked and the place deserted when he arrived to make his routine inspection. His daily search, he said, entailed a visit to every room, and he never failed to inspect the basement and the cellars. After he had completed his tour, finding nothing unusual in the course of it, he had left the Bedford Tower, testing the front door after he closed it to make certain it was locked.

On the Friday evening, he said, it had been shortly after a quarter past seven when he arrived at the Office of Arms. Once again he had carried out his inspection. Passing through the library he had noted that the handle of the safe was in the closed position, so he had not tested it; but, as was customary when he went through Stivey's room, he had tried the door of the strong-room and found it locked. Then, at about 7.30, he had let himself out of the Office, again checking that the front door was locked behind him.

7

While the police were thus engaged, Vicars and his guest, fortified by breakfast, set off for the Castle. Probably they made the journey in Ulster's carriage driven by the suspect though unsuspecting Phillips. On their arrival they found that Kerr was waiting to question Vicars. Goldney, in whom the police were not interested, probably retired to Ulster's room, for he was not present during the ensuing interview which took place in the library.

Kerr made no reference to Mrs Farrell's information but, instead, he asked Vicars to tell him all that occurred before he left the Office on the Friday evening. In doing this, Ulster confirmed Stivey's story. He then went on to say that after the messenger had gone home, he had found it necessary to go more than once to the telephone (which must have been installed in the messenger's room) and, in doing so, had passed each time the door of the strong-room. Had the handle not been in the correct, closed position, he would certainly have noticed it. Vicars was sure that Stivey had locked the strong-room properly. Even then, it would appear, Kerr said nothing of Mrs Farrell's discoveries.

Vicars thought it had been about ten minutes past seven when he and Horlock were ready to leave. As they reached the foot of the staircase, he had turned to his secretary.

'Wait a minute,' he had told him, 'till I make my usual tour of inspection.'

Going into the library he had walked the length of the room, satisfying himself that all the doors of the bookcases were closed. Then, passing through the second door which connects the library with the messenger's room, he glanced up to see that the window was properly bolted, tried the handle of the strong-room and, reassured that all was well, had joined Horlock in the hall.

It was this accustomed tour which had probably earned for Vicars his reputation for fussiness. Yet never, it would appear, did he change his routine to cross the floor of the library and try the handle of the safe, even when he knew that his own key to the front door was missing, even when he knew that the front door had been found open.

As Vicars and Horlock stepped out of the Office of Arms they found waiting for them a well-known Dublin journalist, a reporter on one of the Irish papers. He was seeking details regarding some particular aspect of the approaching royal visit, but found to his surprise that he was better informed on the point than was Vicars himself. Listening to the journalist's story, Vicars decided that he must telephone immediately to Viceregal Lodge.

To do this, the obvious course would have been for him to open the door he had just locked and use the telephone in Stivey's room. But Vicars knew that the operator in charge of the Castle switchboard would have gone off duty for the night, leaving the individual lines, such as that of the Office of Arms, switched through to the Dublin exchange. From long experience Ulster was well aware of the boredom and the delays which would be his if he should attempt to reach Viceregal Lodge from that instrument. He therefore decided that it would save both time and trouble to use the telephone in the Chief Secretary's Office, which was connected directly with the Lord-Lieutenant's residence. Having made sure once more that the door of the Bedford Tower was locked, he said good-night to the journalist and Mr Horlock and walked across to the Chief Secretary's Office on the other side of Upper Castle Yard.

Scarcely had the three men separated and gone their several ways than the conscientious Kerr arrived to make his nightly inspection of the premises and to find, as on so many other occasions, that all was, so far as he could see, exactly as it should be.

By half-past seven – at which time Kerr believed he had left the Office of Arms – Vicars had finished his telephone conversation and directed his steps towards the Kildare Street Club. His stay there must, however, have been very brief as he was in his own house in St James's Terrace before eight o'clock when dinner was announced.

It must have taken Kerr a considerable time to lead Vicars through this detailed account of the previous Friday; and, at some point during their conversation, they moved from the

library to Stivey's room. It was there, standing together outside
the strong-room, that the detective first mentioned Mrs Farrell.

'It is a wonder,' he remarked, 'that you didn't report the
finding of the door of the strong-room open on the Saturday
morning, even after the Jewels had been missed.'

'Oh,' said Vicars, 'I was so thronged owing to the preparing
for the King's visit.'

And that was to sum up his attitude throughout the whole
long-drawn-out investigation. He simply could not understand
that there was anything either strange or suspicious in his not
having told the police about Mrs Farrell's discoveries.

Later that Monday, when questioned on the same matter by
Sir John Ross, he explained that he had been so upset by the
theft that he had entirely forgotten about the door of the strong-
room having been found open.

Poor Kerr, understandably baffled by Ulster's unconcern,
now brought the conversation back to the vexed question of the
keys and their holders. When he was giving evidence before the
Commission of Inquiry six months later, Kerr was to say that,
on that Monday morning, Vicars produced from his pocket *two*
latch-keys to the front door.

'This,' Vicars is said to have told the detective, 'is one that I
got from Mr Mahony, and this is another one that I mislaid. *I
discovered that this morning.*'

No member of the Commission recognised the importance of
the discrepancy which then emerged between the detective's
statement and that made previously by Vicars, who declared
that it was not until the morning of the 9th or 10th July, that he
found upon his dressing-table the key which he had lost.

There are other indications that Kerr's memory, usually reliable enough, was not entirely trustworthy. He stated that later
that day, when making a particular search of the premises, he saw
'Sir Arthur Vicars take a key out of a roll of cloth or paper,
saturated with oil, which was in a glass case or locked drawer in
the strong-room. Sir Arthur Vicars said, "This is the fourth key."
The detective went on to say that he '*felt quite certain*' that
Vicars had then explained to him that 'Mr Mahony's key is also
in the strong-room. He did not keep possession of it ... He gave
it to me, and I deposited it in the strong-room when going on
holidays.' According to his own account Kerr then asked why,

since Mahony had now returned to Dublin, he had not taken possession of his keys. Stivey took it upon himself to explain.

'Though he is back,' he said, 'he has not taken to work yet. He only puts in an appearance for an hour or two, and that is why he left early on Friday evening. He merely puts in an appearance in the afternoon.'

From which it is clear that this conversation must have taken place on the Saturday and not, as Kerr stated, on the following Monday. It is known that, on previous occasions, Mahony had left his keys with his uncle when he went on holiday and, on that dreadful Saturday, Vicars may have supposed mistakenly that his nephew had done this before he went to England; but it is most improbable that Vicars would have made such a mistake on the Monday, when Mahony had handed him his keys on the Saturday evening and he had them in his pocket at that moment. A further inaccuracy in Kerr's evidence was his statement that the fourth key to the strong-room was taken from a glass case or locked drawer in that room. It was well established that the keys in the strong-room were kept in an unlocked drawer; one, in fact, which could not be locked.

8

Although reluctant to suspect Vicars, Kerr's superiors were forced, after studying the detective's report, to admit that there were some matters touching the King of Arms which were, to say the very least, most unsatisfactory.

First, there was the undeniable fact that he was the only person known to have in his possession a key that would open the safe. Indeed, he held the only two known to exist. Secondly, there was the extraordinary manner in which he received the news, both on the Wednesday and the Saturday, that Mrs Farrell had found open doors which should have been securely closed. On neither occasion did he check that the Jewels were safe; and this scarcely tallied with his story that his custody of the insignia was a constant source of anxiety to him. Thirdly, there was his failure to tell the police of Mrs Farrell's discoveries when they questioned him on the Saturday. Fourthly, there was that curious story, freely admitted by Vicars, that he had thought it more convenient to go to the Chief Secretary's office to telephone to Viceregal Lodge than to return to his own office, which he had only just left.

The police were bound to consider whether this last incident might not have been a carefully planned ruse to enable Vicars to leave the Bedford Tower while Kerr carried out his inspection and then, when the detective had gone, to return to the Office of Arms, rifle the safe at his leisure and, carrying his spoils, walk out of the Castle and dispose of the insignia as he would.

Already the police had taken a number of obvious steps. They had asked Scotland Yard to send an officer to Dublin to help them in their enquiries. They were busily compiling a detailed description of the missing objects and would circulate this to police forces throughout the world. They had already been in touch with the makers of the safe to discover how the door had been opened. Inquiries were being made among the locksmiths of the city to find out whether any keys, capable of opening either the safe or the door of the strong-room, had been cut during recent months. Now, however, the authorities began to investigate more closely the statements made by Vicars.

At once they found themselves confronted with that recurrent phenomenon, the invisibility of the familiar. During the previous fourteen years Ulster had become so much a part of the Dublin scene that, when the detectives questioned the sentries and police who had been on duty on the Friday, not one of them could be certain that he had seen Vicars on that evening, whether leaving the Castle or within the precincts of Upper Castle Yard. Similarly, when the staff of the Kildare Street Club were interrogated, no one could be found to confirm or deny Vicars' assertion that he had called there on his way home. Not until the police went to St James's Terrace did they meet with any support for Ulster's story. Both his housekeeper and Pitt, the footman, were prepared to swear that their employer arrived home on the Friday night before dinner was served at eight o'clock.

From this it appeared that, if Kerr was right in saying that he had left the Office of Arms at half past seven, Vicars would have had no more than thirty minutes to return to the Bedford Tower from the Chief Secretary's office, to open the safe and abstract the Jewels, taking time and care to remove the fragment of blue ribbon, to fold the tissue and silver paper away in the rifled cases before stacking these neatly back in the safe and then, if there was any truth in these suppositions, walked away with the regalia. And then called at his club?

The police estimated that, had Vicars taken a cab from the Castle to the Club, the journey would have occupied seven or eight minutes and that, had he taken another from the Club to his house, a further ten minutes would have been absorbed. Would anyone, with such great issues at stake, have formed a plan that required so much to be done in so short a time? And would Vicars, or anyone else, have dared to bank upon the chance that no one, either among the staff or the members, would be able to state categorically that Ulster had been, or had not been, in the Club that evening? The more they considered the whole proposition, the more improbable it seemed that Vicars could have carried out the theft, at any rate in the way that had been suggested.

But was it necessary, someone asked, that the theft had been committed on the Friday night? Was there any reason why it should have been perpetrated on that day rather than any of the others which had elapsed since 11th June, when Vicars had shown the Jewels to Mr Hodgson? After all, were there not indications that the thief had become impatient that the theft had remained so long undiscovered? Was this the real significance of those doors being found unlocked? Did the thief, having obtained possession of the Jewels, wish to precipitate the discovery of the theft? But why? Could it be, for instance, that a carefully planned alibi would be of no avail if the disappearance of the Jewels remained any longer unnoticed? Did this indicate that the thief was not, ostensibly at least, in Ireland when the theft was committed? If there was anything in this line of reasoning, then Vicars must be cleared of suspicion. Had he taken such elaborate steps to court discovery, he would have called in the police as soon as Mrs Farrell's adventures were reported to him. Yet why had he chosen this Saturday, of all days, to give the key of the safe to Stivey?

Over and over again, backwards and forwards, the discussions continued. Each new theory, when studied carefully, gave rise to considerations which, for one reason or another, seemed to render it untenable.

While their superiors debated these matters, the detectives were continuing their inquiries among the police and the sentries, the staff of the Kildare Street Club and anyone else who might know something, have seen something, which could give a new and more promising direction to the investigation.

On the Monday the Dublin representative of the Milner Safe Company was asked to examine the door and the lock of the strong-room. With the exasperating precision of the trained mechanic, Mr F. J. O'Hare took the lock to pieces and removed from it the seven levers which were set in motion when the key was inserted and turned in the two keyholes of the door. Upon the highly polished surfaces of these levers he found no trace of anything that might suggest that the door had been tampered with in any way.

Next day Mr Cornelius Gallagher, an employee of Messrs Ratner's agents in Dublin, performed a similar examination of the safe. He also removed the lock, extracted the various levers and found nothing unusual about them.

Both these experts agreed that the locks had not been picked, nor had any attempt been made to pick them. They were also convinced that the locks had been opened only by their own keys—or by others so exactly identical that they left no trace—and that such keys could not have been fabricated from a wax impression. Had they been so, although they might have opened the locks, visible signs of friction or of pressure must have been left upon the mirror-like surfaces of the levers.

Once again the pointer of suspicion turned towards Vicars; but he, completely oblivious of the doubts harboured by the police regarding himself, asked only to be left in peace in order that he might complete the arrangements for the royal visit, now only two days away. So, as soon as he was at liberty to do so, he escaped to the comparative peace of his own room, where Frank Goldney was waiting for him. There, for the greater part of what remained of the working day, the two men strove to unravel the last problems of protocol and procedure.

At about three o'clock in the afternoon, just as Vicars was preparing to leave, two police officers were ushered into his room by Stivey. They announced that they had orders to search the whole building thoroughly and wished Vicars to be present while they did so. He told them that this was out of the question as he must leave at once to keep an appointment with the Lord-Lieutenant at Viceregal Lodge. He promised, however, that he would meet them on the following morning at half-past ten, when he would give them all the assistance he could. Then, leaving Goldney to find his own way home but arranging to join him there before dinner, Vicars drove to his meeting with the Lord-Lieutenant.

Seldom, perhaps, can Lord Aberdeen have displayed his natural kindliness to better effect than on this occasion. It would have been so easy for him to upbraid Vicars for permitting such a catastrophe to overwhelm the viceregal world, particularly at this most unpropitious time. Instead, he would seem to have infused into Vicars at least some of the optimism with which, so surprisingly, he himself viewed the affair at that moment.

For when he returned to the Castle from Viceregal Lodge, Vicars was in a more hopeful frame of mind than he had been at any time since the theft had been discovered. Kerr was still on duty in the Office of Arms and, immediately after he arrived there, Vicars told him that he was now quite persuaded that the whole business was no more than an elaborate practical joke.

'I would not be a bit surprised,' he told Kerr, 'that they [the Jewels and collars] would be returned to my house by parcel post tomorrow morning. His Excellency, this evening, said the same thing.'

Upon which note of hope, more nearly approaching gaiety, perhaps, than anything else in this story, Vicars departed to spend the evening with his friend, Frank Bennett-Goldney.

9

During this time one member of Ulster's heraldic court was still in England. Shackleton had been invited to spend that week-end, the last before he returned to Ireland for the installation ceremony, with his friends, Lord Ronald Sutherland-Gower and Mr Frank Hird.

Lord Ronald Gower was, throughout his life, to be the victim of two strains in his personality violently opposed to each other. On one hand he was the eleventh and youngest child of the second Duke of Sutherland, with no less than three duchesses among his four sisters; on the other, he was endowed with considerable artistic ability and is still sometimes remembered as the creator of the Shakespeare Memorial at Stratford-on-Avon. A would-be Bohemian bred in that rigid, class-conscious group composed of the very rich members of the British aristocracy of his period, it is scarcely surprising that, early in 1907 at the age of 62, these two warring elements brought on a severe attack of epilepsy. In consequence, he was ordered to lead a very quiet life indeed, and retired to Hammerfield, the house he had purchased at Penshurst in 1899 in the belief that 'it would be the very thing for Frank and myself.'[1] Fortunately he had in Mr Frank Hird a devoted companion. They had met in 1893, when the latter was the Rome correspondent of the *Morning Post*. Drawn together by their mutual interests, they became so deeply attached that, in 1898, Lord Ronald had taken the unusual step of adopting Mr Hird as his legal son.

Lord Ronald's family, however, remained loyal; and among those who never faltered in their tolerant affection for him was his nephew, the Duke of Argyll.

Between them existed a life-long bond. The Duchess of Sutherland and her eldest daughter Lady Lorne, afterwards Duchess of Argyll, were brought to bed of fine sons at Stafford House, the Sutherlands' London home, at about the same time. With that regard for precedence which is second nature to those born in ducal circles, Her Grace of Sutherland was delivered of Lord Ronald Gower five days before Lady Lorne gave birth to Queen Victoria's future son-in-law. It is scarcely surprising that, despite the widely differing interests that were theirs, uncle and nephew remained very attached to each other.

That the Duke of Argyll should be a fellow-guest at Hammerfield may well have served as a measure by which Frank Shackleton might calculate the distance he had already travelled since the days when, as a schoolboy, he had traversed the suburban roads which lay between his father's house and Dulwich College. But he could never be content with such success as Frank Hird had won for himself. He would be satisfied only when he had amassed the solid backing of wealth for which he had already worked so hard.

---

[1] Lord R. S. Gower, *Old Diaries* (John Murray, London), p. 364.

During those agreeable, seemingly carefree days he spent at Penshurst, there must have been moments when, in imagination, Shackleton was transported far from the civilised beauties of that very English house with its white-painted balconies and gables, its well-kept gardens, to the tropical forests of Mexico, where exotic birds and butterflies swooped and hovered.

If only the last few stages in his plans might be completed, if only he and his associates could raise the capital needed to secure the concessions upon which he had already obtained options, work could begin and his future would be assured.

On the Monday morning, the Duke of Argyll and Shackleton travelled together to London by train. It was the Duke who, opening *The Times* as the train resumed its journey, read out to his companion the news that the Irish Crown Jewels had disappeared. There will have been no dearth of material for conversation during the remainder of their journey.

Shackleton drove to one of his clubs and found Vicars' telegram asking him to go to Scotland Yard. On his arrival he was taken at once to Chief Inspector John Kane, the officer who had been selected to go to Ireland to investigate the mystery. It is clear that, at their first interview, Kane formed a very favourable and lasting impression of Shackleton.

When Kane had completed his questions about the Office of Arms and those who worked there, Shackleton must have gone to his flat in Park Lane to prepare for his visit to Ireland. Later he caught the boat-train on which he had already reserved a sleeping compartment.

As a man of developed social awareness he will probably have glanced at the list of persons also travelling that evening in reserved accommodation; and, if he did, the surprise and pleasure he showed when he met Lady Ormonde [1] and her daughter, Lady Constance Butler, on the boat next morning, may not have been quite so spontaneous as was theirs on seeing him.

'Oh, Mr Shackleton,' cried Lady Ormonde, 'how extraordinary! Poor Sir Arthur, I am sorry for him! Isn't it an odd thing? Constance and I were just talking. We were just saying how odd it was, that remark of yours at lunch the other day.'

[1] Daughter of the 1st Duke of Westminster by his wife, a daughter of the 2nd Duke of Sutherland. Married the 3rd Marquess of Ormonde, 1876, and died in 1928.

It had been made at a luncheon party she had given at her house in Upper Brook Street on the previous Thursday, 4th July. At table the conversation had turned to Vicars; and some-one ventured to criticise him for attaching altogether too much importance to his post. They had even described his painstaking interest in his work as 'fussiness'. Shackleton had at once leapt to Ulster's defence.

'But he has a great deal of responsibility,' he pointed out, 'and he is very proud of his Office.'

Lady Ormonde had adroitly turned the conversation from the personal to the impersonal, from Vicars to the Crown Jewels.

'Oh, I should not be surprised,' Shackleton remarked of these, 'to hear that they were stolen some day.'

These were the words which Lady Ormonde remembered. These were the words which were to be repeated, over and over again, in the clubs and great houses which, with ever-increasing assurance, Shackleton liked to regard as his natural surround-ings. At this time, however, it never occurred to him that he might have said, and he so rarely did, the wrong thing. After all, not every prophet sees his forecast proved true within forty-eight hours.

On their arrival in Dublin Shackleton drove to St James's Terrace, where he found Vicars still in bed. Their meeting on this occasion did not follow the usual pattern which the two friends had established over the years. No gossip now of mutual friends, no tales of triumphs won. Vicars appeared to be com-pletely overwhelmed by the disaster which had enveloped him. He was not even able to talk very much about the robbery.

This dramatic alteration from the optimism which he had showed upon his return from Viceregal Lodge on the previous evening must have been due to the influence of Mr Goldney. It appears that Goldney, contrary to the hopes which had inspired Vicars to ask him to arrive a day earlier than had been planned, had proved to be no real help in Ulster's appalling dilemma. Instead, he had lost no opportunity of pointing out the disastrous consequences which must ensue for everyone connected with the Office of Arms if the Jewels were not recovered immediately.

Shackleton, whose natural buoyancy was no small part of his professional stock in trade, attempted to persuade Vicars to take a more sanguine view of the situation, that he should at least wait until the arrival of the parcel post before plunging himself and his friends into so deep a slough of despond; but very soon he had to confess himself defeated. So, leaving Vicars, he retired to the bedroom where Goldney was shaving; and it was from him that Shackleton learnt the details of the robbery and some of the measures subsequently taken by the police.

10

Meanwhile, at breakfast tables all over Great Britain, people were learning for the first time the extraordinary story of the disappearance of the Crown Jewels.

The Times pointed out that the regalia would appear to have been as carefully guarded against theft as anything could well be.

> Just round the corner of the building a soldier and a policeman are on duty day and night, and a few yards away, at the entrance, is the Chief Secretary's office, where another police man is stationed during office hours. The headquarters of the Dublin Metropolitan Police, the headquarters of the Dublin detective force, the headquarters of the Royal Irish Constabulary and the head office of the Dublin military garrison are all within a radius of 50 yards of the Office of Arms. In a word, there is no spot in Dublin, or possibly in the United Kingdom, which is at all hours of the twenty-four more constantly and systematically occupied by soldiers and policemen. . . . It is understood, however, that up to this evening [July 8th] the police were without a clue.

The *Daily Graphic*, under bold headlines, THE STOLEN INSIGNIA, carried a picture of the Jewels copied from that in Burke's *Peerage*. This was followed by an account of the theft calculated to arouse the most lively curiosity among the readers of the paper. The writer had probably been sent over from London to cover the royal visit, for he seems to have been quite unprepared for the lack of co-operation extended to the Press by the officials at Dublin Castle. Any journalist would regard the disappearance of the Jewels as a story infinitely more worth the telling than would be the recital of just another royal occasion with its glimpses of gracious condescension, of memories as remarkable as those of retentive elephants, of addresses presented and bouquets received; but the viceregal staff showed themselves totally unaware of the needs of the British public. As a result the *Graphic* sought to retaliate by suggesting that important information was being withheld by the authorities.

> A profound sensation [it said] has been caused in Dublin and a feeling akin to consternation in official circle at the disappearance from Dublin Castle of State Jewels belonging to the Order of St Patrick. The greatest reticence has been maintained in the matter. Every effort was made to prevent the news becoming public. . . . If they [the authorities] are in possession of any clue they have closely kept the information to themselves.

He then went on to imply that the Jewels were not nearly as valuable as the Viceregal Court would have the world believe.

> Estimates as to what they are really worth have been exaggerated. They do not represent anything like the money value of £50,000. It is not long since a Dublin jeweller valued the lot at from £16,000 to £17,000. Under £20,000 is a safe estimate. The most valuable parts are the brilliants in the star. . . . If the Jewels are to be replaced, the Crown would doubtless have to pay for them. But, of course, the Order of St Patrick cannot go on without the jewel badge for the Grand Master[1] unless the Grand Master is willing to wear paste, as some Lords-Lieutenant have done who did not care for the responsibility of carrying the original article.
>
> The safe is said to have been a very old one. . . . The Jewels in the little room were not watched over with any special care, Dublin being accustomed to honesty.

There would seem to have been something almost in the nature of a conspiracy to proclaim Dublin innocent of any part in the crime which had been perpetrated within its Castle walls. In London, according to another paragraph in the same paper, an official spokesman had said:

> Dublin is not quite such a den of thieves as London. Certainly Irish people have been trusted to pass in and out of the Bermingham Tower of Dublin Castle freely and two generations of Irishmen have not abused the liberty. In fact, the present theft is not put down to Dublin at all. That it was cleverly planned in London is hardly doubted.

To the Nationalist Members of Parliament, ever on the alert to

---

[1] There was no basis in fact for this statement.

embarrass the British Government, whatever its political com-
plexion, the news of the theft came as a gift from heaven. It
mattered nothing to them whether the Jewels were recovered or
not, but they recognised with glee an opportunity to administer
a drawn-out series of pinpricks to the Irish Secretary. The first
of the many questions which were to be asked on the subject in
the House of Commons was put on that Monday, the day on
which the news of the robbery reached London. 'Mr Patrick
O'Brien jumped up and asked, 'How many police were guarding
the Crown Jewels when they were stolen from Dublin Castle?'
No answer was given by Mr Birrell[1], but a loud laugh went up
from both sides of the House.'

11

Meanwhile, as the public read avidly through the pages devoted
in every journal that Tuesday morning to the disappearance of
the Jewels, the three heraldic bachelors gathered at the breakfast
table in St James's Terrace.

The ebullient Shackleton, refreshed by his bath and feeling it
his duty to dissolve, if he could, the encircling gloom which
surrounded both Ulster and Goldney, set himself to amuse his
older companions. He believed that an account of his meeting
on the boat with Lady Ormonde and Lady Constance Butler
could scarcely fail to charm a smile from the disgruntled Vicars.
In this, however, he could not have been more mistaken.

As he recounted his story and explained all that had passed at
the luncheon party in Upper Brook Street, Vicars, more fretted
than the other realised by the growing tension of the past few
days, could not conceal his annoyance. In his present state of
mind, Shackleton's casual remark about the likelihood of the
Jewels being stolen appeared to be no better than a calculated
stab in the back.

'Well, if you thought they were unsafe,' he demanded, 'why
did you not ever speak to me?'

Goldney, wise after the event, chose to admonish Shackleton.

'Why did you think they were unsafe?' he asked. 'And why
did you say such an extraordinary thing at such a peculiar time?'

[1] Augustine Birrell (1850–1933); politician and man of letters. Irish Secretary,
1907–16.

With commendable restraint Shackleton ignored the silliness implicit in Goldney's second question and replied to the first.

'Because the Office was left at night and because it was so lonely.'

At half past nine Shackleton and Goldney presented themselves at the Office of Arms to be questioned by the police. They may have carried with them a message from Vicars to explain why he could not keep punctually the appointment he had made with the two police officers. Certainly they could not have expected him to arrive at the Castle much later than themselves, or the officers, who must have had plenty to do elsewhere in connection with the case, would scarcely have remained there, doing nothing. In the end, however, Vicars kept them waiting until half-past twelve, two hours later than he had arranged.

But when, at last, he did reach the Office, and although he remained with the police while they made what must have proved for Vicars a most exasperating search of the premises, he does not appear to have offered any explanation as to why he was so late. In the end, after they had gone so far as to take down a wall behind which, according to their careful measurements, a cavity existed, the police had to admit themselves baffled.

There is, we believe, a simple explanation to account for Vicars' failure to keep his appointment. Despite all that Goldney had said to dampen his hopes, his innate optimism was not yet dead. He still believed that somehow, somewhere, he would find a happy issue out of all his troubles. So, although the police were expecting him, and the precious moments were slipping by, and very soon the royal yacht would be steaming to its appointed moorings at Kingstown, he had waited at home until there no longer remained any possibility that the parcel post would bring to him that morning the missing regalia.

Only when his optimism had seeped away, when he finally recognised that he had been made the victim of a monstrous conspiracy, did he leave his home, walking down that wide flight of steps into a familiar, seemingly unchanged world of urban summer. But as he drove through the streets, as he acknowledged the salutes of sentries and police at the Castle gates and outside the Office of Arms, Vicars began to understand that, for him, nothing would ever be quite the same again.

BOOK TWO

The Investigation

CHAPTER ONE

1

At four o'clock on the morning of Wednesday, 10th July, as the first light of dawn began to show in the eastern sky, the *Victoria and Albert*, the supreme elegance of its lines so oddly at variance with the picture of regal domesticity invoked by its name, entered Kingstown Harbour. Four hours later the peace of the summer morning was shattered by the crash of a royal salute. Already the crowds were gathering along the route Their Majesties would take. Indeed this day was to witness the most spectacular welcome ever given by the Irish people to an English sovereign. So impressed by this was the correspondent of *The Times* that he wrote :

> Fortunately it has ceased to be necessary to speculate about the nature of the King's reception by his Irish subjects.

Although Lord Aberdeen would not have entirely agreed with this view, he was more immediately concerned about another matter as, at noon, a launch carried him across the sparkling water towards the yacht. He has left his own account of that uneasy meeting.

'As soon as the King had shaken hands, I was conscious that he was scrutinising the badge of the Order of St Patrick which I was wearing. I was afraid it might have been incorrectly placed, and said, "Is it not right, sir?" "Oh yes," said the King, "but I was thinking of those Jewels."' Lord Aberdeen tells how King Edward 'very considerately did not allude to the subject again during that visit, but there was plenty of discussion on the unwelcome topic consequently.[1]'

Nothing could demonstrate more clearly how well King Edward deserved his title of 'The Peacemaker' than does this example of his remarkable self-restraint. For in his official bio-

[1] *More Cracks with 'We Twa'*, by the Marquess and Marchioness of Aberdeen & Temair (Methuen & Co., London, 1929), pp. 142–3.

graphy of the King, Sir Sidney Lee shows that His Majesty was by no means unmoved by the loss of his Irish diamonds.

'The King' (he wrote) 'was in Dublin when he learnt the particulars of the theft, and his language on that occasion was vigorous and forceful, partly for reason that in the particular circumstances he could do nothing and partly because of the feeble efforts that were being made to elucidate the mystery.[1]'

The waiting crowds on the shore were steadily increasing. Undoubtedly interest in the royal visit had been heightened by the news of the robbery, and the morning papers carried two official announcements calculated to fan both gossip and speculation.

The investiture of Lord Castletown was to be postponed; and the Government stated that one thousand pounds would be paid for information leading to the recovery of the Jewels and the capture of the thief or thieves. For among the crowd, bred in an Ireland where poverty was a part of the very fabric of life, few would have dared to prophecy that, after more than fifty years, such a reward would remain unclaimed.

Immediately after Lord Aberdeen had returned to the shore, the royal party embarked in a steam pinnace which brought them to Victoria Wharf where they were received by the Lord Lieutenant and Lady Aberdeen. Then, after various presentations had been made and the King had inspected the guard of honour, that odd exercise in mutual embarrassment and self-consciousness which is inseparable from any royal occasion, Their Majesties and Princess Victoria entered the state carriage. Then, amid a flurry of dust, the royal party drove between cheering crowds along 'The Rocky Road to Dublin', a wave of gloved hands, the gracious doffing of a silk hat, making acknowledgment of the people's welcome.

When they reached the Exhibition at Ballsbridge, Their Majesties carried out their expected duties with that genial aloofness which is not the least remarkable of the qualities distinguishing the royal house of Great Britain. King Edward made an impressive figure in a frock coat embellished with an immense white carnation, a silk hat and a black silk stock secured by a very large pearl pin. The gold watch-chain draped across

[1] *King Edward VII*, by Sir Sidney Lee (Macmillan & Co., London, 1927), Vol. II, p. 474.

his stomach was as individual as were the dark gloves, their backs ornamented with broad lines of stitching, which he was wearing. For her part, Queen Alexandra looked charming in a severely tailored dress of black and white striped silk with Irish lace on the bodice, the skirt cut very full at the back and so long that it touched the ground. A ruched and flowered boa reached far below the Queen's tiny waist, and she wore a small hat of green straw with a wreath of pink roses. There was about her that faint air of unreality which appeared inseparable from many royal ladies of her generation.

Lady Aberdeen had been less fortunate in her choice of a hat, for hers was a large round confection garnished with long maize-coloured feathers and worn perfectly straight above her round, good-natured face. It did match, however, her costume of striped brown satin, which was enlivened with brown crêpe-de-chine and lace. Her kindly smile and tall, stout figure, with its rounded back and sloping shoulders, suggest that any trouble, whether of State or household, would soon slide off to be replaced by a tranquil cheerfulness.

From the Exhibition the royal party drove to Viceregal Lodge to attend a large garden party, where Queen Alexandra was able to see some of Lady Aberdeen's little terriers. Later they returned to Kingstown by motor-car and were taken out to their yacht. Not for long, however, was to be their respite from official duties. As the evening drew on and, on the ships of the royal escort, illuminations and fireworks split the summer dusk, sixteen guests arrived for dinner.

One feels that, although the King may have refrained from mentioning the disappearance of his jewels when the Aberdeens were within earshot, he must, to others, have expressed his feelings upon the subject with a vehemence made infinitely more formidable by his guttural accent.

Very possibly Lady Ormonde was granted an opportunity on that evening to tell the King of the very odd thing – it now seemed quite prophetic – which Mr Shackleton had said at her luncheon party during the previous week. She may also have mentioned having met him on the Irish boat when he was returning to Dublin after spending the previous week-end with her uncle, Lord Ronald Gower, and that the King's brother-in-law and her cousin, the Duke of Argyll, had also been of the party at

Hammerfield. For it is certain that the King early learnt that
the Duke of Argyll was on friendly terms with Mr Shackleton.

How Vicars spent that long, for him unhappy, day is not known.
Probably he was among the fifty-four guests who sat down to
luncheon with Their Majesties in the Grand Palace Restaurant
at the Exhibition; and he doubtless made an appearance at the
viceregal garden party; but we have found no mention of him
nor of his attendant heralds in any of the accounts we have read
of that day's activities.

We know, however, that Goldney left Dublin that evening.
His hopes of attending upon the King during Lord Castletown's
investiture had been shattered by the cancellation of that ceremony; and he was probably only too glad to escape as soon as
possible from the house in St James's Terrace. It was not that
either Vicars or Shackleton did anything to make their guest
feel unwelcome. That was, in fact, the very last thing they wished
to do. It was simply that they never realised that their talk of
mutual friends and common interests, gossip of the little world
they had shared during the past few years, only served to accen-
tuate that sense of haunting loneliness which drove Goldney on
in his efforts to impress all those who – or so it seemed to him –
withheld from him their friendship. He had done so much for
Vicars, yet Ulster seemed to prefer Shackleton, a man whom
Goldney suspected was by no means trustworthy. The thought
of Mother and the mayoral duties awaiting him at Canterbury
drew him homewards.

2

Chief Inspector Kane exhibited no urgent desire to reach the
scene of the crime he had been chosen to investigate. Probably,
being Irish himself, he felt that no one at Dublin Castle would
give him their undivided attention so long as the King and
Queen were there. It was not until 12th July, that Kane and
his men reported to the Dublin Metropolitan Police.

In the interval, however, he had not been idle. Descriptions
of the missing Jewels had been sent to police forces throughout

the world. A close check had been made into the recent activities of all criminals whose records suggested that they might have been involved in this spectacular larceny. Steps had been taken to ensure that Scotland Yard would be notified immediately if the diamonds were offered for sale on the London market. It was still hoped that the offer of a reward might encourage someone to bring forward some useful information. Nevertheless, when Kane and his party left London, no clue of any kind had been discovered.

Kane, however, was by no means despondent. He had had time to study very carefully the reports forwarded to London by the Dublin police. These, with the information given to him by Shackleton, had helped him to form a very clear picture of the Office of Arms and the daily routine of those who worked there. Like Sir John Ross, Kane had been puzzled and fascinated by the fragment of blue silk ribbon which had been removed from the Badge with such meticulous care. Although he did not agree with Vicars that this operation would have taken at least ten minutes, he regarded the ribbon as proof positive that the jewels had been stolen either by someone having a legitimate right of entry to the Bedford Tower, or by someone introduced to the Office of Arms by a member of the staff at a time when their tampering with the safe and its contents would not be noticed. As he was to explain to Vicars at their first meeting:

'The thief was in no hurry to leave the premises,' he observed. 'If my opinion is worth anything, this gentleman [Lowe] must remain to look for the thief in this building, because what he has described to me would be utterly impossible, to my mind, on the part of an ordinary or outside thief.'

But Vicars refused to accept this suggestion.

'I have,' he said, 'implicit confidence in every member of my staff.'

Throughout his stay in Dublin, Kane was haunted by the memory of a report he had been shown before he left London. This represented the findings of a group of officers who had been investigating the activities of some well-known homosexuals. In the course of their researches they had found that several members of this masculine coven had, when in Ireland, been in touch with Vicars. This did not necessarily mean that Ulster was one of those; but the Wilde case had demonstrated all too clearly how vulnerable to blackmail are men of this kind. And Kane, with his long experience of the London underworld, was well aware that a pervert, whether baulked of his prey or wounded in his brittle vanity, can prove at least as dangerous as any woman. It was these considerations which led him to declare that the Jewels had been taken at this particular juncture 'because there was a certain high personage coming here, and possibly certain people thought that, when these Jewels disappeared, it would be necessary that some explanation of that should be forthcoming before their arrival'.

Unfortunately it is now impossible to discover along what lines Kane and his men worked while they were in Ireland. Certainly they were a great deal more successful than were the Dublin police; for within a few days of his arrival, Kane submitted to Sir John Ross a report on his investigations. This named the person whom Kane believed had been responsible for the disappearance of the Crown Jewels. For reasons which must have seemed of extreme importance to the authorities, Kane's identification of the thief proved quite unacceptable, and he and his men were returned to Scotland Yard without further ado. As the *Gaelic American* told its readers on 4th July, 1908:

> Several detectives were brought over from Scotland Yard. After a few days they unravelled the mystery and the case was promptly taken out of their hands. The Scotland Yard men found out too much and were sent home at once. To find out more than is wanted is a very bad thing for a detective to do in a case of this sort. The matter was again in the hands of the Dublin police.

Exhaustive inquiries in both London and Dublin have failed to trace either Kane's report, or that which dealt with the activities of the fashionable Edwardian perverts. Unfortunately, when the British authorities handed over power to the Free State Government, many documents tending to discredit the English were destroyed. Others, which might serve to identify those among the Irish who acted as Government informers, were placed under an interdict which prevents their publication until after the year 2022. The reasons for this are understandable; but it does not facilitate the study of recent Irish history.

It must, however, have been on Kane's instructions that, on the day he arrived in Dublin, Sergeant Sheehan obtained from

Vicars the first signed statement he had been asked to make. This followed very closely the information he had already given to Harrel and to Kerr; but it may be helpful to run over some of the points contained in this document.

'I am in charge,' Vicars told Sheehan, 'of the Office of Arms, Dublin Castle. The Jewels were last cleaned about the end of January 1907, in the strong-room, the grille being locked during the time they were cleaning them . . . and were carefully examined by me, and I took possession of them from the men.

'The Jewels were last worn by His Excellency on 15th March, 1907. After which I brought them back and placed them in the safe in the library. . . .

'On 11th June I showed the diamonds to Mr J. C. Hodgson, F.S.A. . . . along with one collar. From 11th June to 6th July I have no recollection of seeing the Jewels, nor of having gone to the safe. The gold collars were last worn at the investiture of the Earl of Meath on 14th April, 1905.

'The cases which contained Lord Ormonde's and Lord Howth's collars were not inspected since April 1905, but Lord Mayo's and Lord Enniskillen's were certainly inspected by me within this year.'

Vicars went on to describe why Wests had sent him the late Lord de Ros's collar, and how he had given it to Stivey to place in the safe. Almost immediately afterwards the messenger had told him that he had found the safe open.

'I said "Impossible" (continued Vicars) 'knowing well the great precautions I always took when locking the safe. I then opened the safe which was unlocked, the handle being turned down, which would represent to outside observation that the safe was locked. I removed the case which always contained the Crown diamonds, and my worst fears were aroused by the lightness of the case and the fact that the key was in the lock, which was never so left by me. On opening the case I found the diamond star and badge had been removed, but the badge-ribbon and clasp were placed in the centre, having been removed from the badge. . . . On further examination I found the collars of Lord Mayo, Lord Enniskillen, Lord Ormonde and Lord Howth missing from the cases, and the late Lord Cork's collar and enamelled badge gone from its deal box. . . . The small box containing my mother's jewels . . . was also gone. . . .

'So far as I know there are only two keys for the safe, which are always in my custody. . . . The key of the safe which I use I always carry with me along with other keys on a steel ring, except on full dress nights, when I remove it from the bunch and carry it on a ring of its own in my uniform coat pocket; the other key for the safe I have always kept concealed in my residence. I have never left the safe keys in my office or other place where any person could get possession of them. . . .

'My key of the strong-room I always carry on my watch chain, which is placed under my pillow at night. I recollect leaving the key of the safe in my writing table at my residence about two months ago, but the keys, with safe key included, were brought to me at my office by my servant Frederick Pitt, within an hour. . . .

'Mr McEnnery, junior, of Rooskey House, Dunboyne, stayed in my house for one night, 2nd July. A man named Riley Walker, 19 years of age, stayed at my house for a fortnight in April last and is at present servant with Sir Kildare Burrows, Kildare. He came to my house to learn his duties as footman under my footman, Frederick Pitt. Walker never visited the Office of Arms, nor had he any knowledge of the keys of the safe.

'Arthur Phillips, my coachman, has a wife and four children and resides in Clonskeagh Terrace. He is seven years in my employment. He had access to my keys about eleven months ago and occasionally visited the library in the Office of Arms. He frequently saw the jewel case with me and often saw me go into the Office of Arms with the cases. . . . Mr Burtchaell is in my employment since I took up office. Mr Horlock is in my employment since January last. I engaged him in London and got a high character of him from his clergy. . . .'

After explaining once again how carefully he had checked that the bookcases in the library were locked on the Friday evening, and telling of his meeting with the journalist as he left the Bedford Tower, Vicars went on:

'I do not suggest any single one of my staff had anything to do with it, nor do I suspect my maid-servant or footman, nor any person who slept in my house. My theory is that some person got wax impressions of the keys . . . Having regard to the great precautions taken by me in the custody of the keys, I cannot entertain the idea that the actual key of the safe was utilized by the thieves.'

This statement was submitted by Sheehan to his superiors, who told him that he must now leave for England to prosecute further inquiries.

Vicars was now feeling a good deal happier. This may, in part at least, have been due to the fact that the lugubrious Goldney had left and that Shackleton had agreed to stay on for the present in Dublin. He was proving most helpful, sparing Vicars all the anxieties he could and showing real understanding and sympathy. Vicars even began to hope that everything would soon settle down again, that the Jewels would be found and he himself permitted to resume his comfortable way of life.

It was in this more reconciled mood that, on 13th July, he wrote to Sir George Holmes, whom he still regarded as chiefly responsible for the present unfortunate situation.

'It would be' (Vicars wrote) 'a hasty conclusion to arrive at were I to attribute the loss of the Jewels to the inaction of the Board of Public Works, though I think it probable that, if my requisitions and requirements had been carried out originally, this burglary could not have occurred. . . .

'I remember (and my letters bear it out) particularly asking for a Bramah lock,[1] of which it is impossible to take wax impressions . . .

'It was not until the strong-room was nearly built, and the door fixed, that I then discovered the door was not wide enough to admit the safe, although I had all along pointed out that I wanted the safe to be placed inside.

'None of us here have the least recollection of Mr Robinson or anyone else offering to put the present safe through the window, and my impression is that the bars were affixed to the window by then.[2]

[1] In a requisition made to the Secretary, Board of Works on 1st October, 1902, Vicars asked for, among other things:
  Item 5. Fire and burglar-proof door for strong-room, large enough to admit trolley for books (Bramah – Needs and Co. – lock preferred, if no objection).
[2] Andrew *Robertson*, Assistant Principal Surveyor of Buildings, told the Commission of Inquiry that:
  The strong-room had been completed at least four months before Sir Arthur Vicars said anything about the safe going in – in a letter of 25th April, 1903.

'I urged that a smaller burglar (not fire-proof) safe be supplied in exchange for the one we had . . . but I was informed that the difficulty of expense arose,[1] and I was told (and you yourself in private conversation also said) that a smaller safe would be supplied later that could enter into the strong-room when another Department required a safe could have ours. This, however, was never done.

'. . . I have always felt that the Board did not fully realise the great responsibility I had and were inclined to think that I exaggerated the value of the Jewels entrusted to my care. We now know whether I was exaggerating or not!

'I cannot say that I considered it likely that a robbery of this sort could be perpetrated with policemen on duty just outside the office and a sentry pacing up and down night and day and a detective making a round of the office every night to be assured that all was safe.

'As regards the abstraction of the Jewels it is an absolute mystery to me, for I took the greatest precautions that any human could take and the key of the safe never left my possession . . . and as proof of the confidence I imposed in my own precautions I entrusted our own family jewels to the same repository. What greater proof could be adduced?

'. . . I cannot feel that I have been fairly treated in the matter by the Board of Works, as the question of money always was raised as an obstacle . . . and when one considers that the amount involved could not have exceeded £30, and the old safe handed over as a set-off, it would seem unreasonable that the matter should have been postponed until some other Department required a safe.

[1] In the schedule Vicars submitted in connection with the Annual Estimates, 1904–5, he applied for:
  1. Burglar (not fireproof) Milner Safe for Crown Jewels and Insignia, Order of St Patrick. Outside measurements 48″ × 24″ × 22″ with three movable shelves (No. 20,014 Milner's estimate): present safe, which will not fit into strong room, to be returned.
Attached to this is the Furniture Clerk's Report:
  There is a very large fire and burglar proof safe in the Office, supplied some time ago for this purpose, and if Sir Arthur Vicars required to have it in strong room, he should have given the Board some intimation of it when the door of strong room was being ordered. There is a sentry night and day on duty outside the Office where this safe is and, under the circumstances, I do not think a new one should be supplied. It might be a very long time before such a safe as the old one would be required.

'You yourself and others of your Department assured me more than once of the absolute security of the safe, and I was led to think that this was so, otherwise I would hardly have entrusted our own family jewels to it.

'It was the only office or house in the Castle in which anything of great value was stored, and yet there was no one resident in the building. I made several efforts to alter this and was backed up by Lord Cadogan, but the Treasury refused to sanction any such proposals. . . .'

This letter demonstrates very well Vicars' refusal to face facts; and this, despite the somewhat whining note, is so absolute that it illumines his faintly ridiculous figure with an almost heroic glow. When he wrote this letter he must have known that the expert locksmiths were agreed that the safe could not have been opened with keys made from wax impressions of the originals. He had himself admitted that the keys had, on more than one occasion, been out of his possession, if only for short periods. Yet, with complete sincerity and more in sorrow than in anger, he repeated his belief that all blame for the loss of the Jewels must rest with the Board of Works.

That the King and the British public should, in the absence of any arrest being made, demand that a scapegoat be provided is understandable. That Vicars should be cast for that ignominious part was, under the circumstances, almost inevitable. But when it was realised that he was quite unable to believe that anyone could seriously hold him responsible for the loss of the Jewels he believed he had always guarded so zealously, the authorities in Dublin Castle, aware that they were not entirely guiltless themselves, came to their inexcusable decision. No selected scapegoat should ever present to the world an appearance of dignity, of harbouring within itself complete faith in the justice of its cause. Because of this, more than for any other reason perhaps, Vicars was to be treated rather as a quarry to be hunted than as a victim to be prepared for sacrifice; and it is typical of life's irony that of all those who were concerned in the sorry, sordid sequel, Vicars alone, despite his manifold shortcomings, leaves us with an impression not devoid of greatness.

3

In the more hopeful mood which had drawn him on to write to Sir George Holmes, Vicars granted an interview to a journalist from the *Daily Express*. An account of this appeared in the issue of 15th July; and the resilience of Ulster's feelings is clearly evident. In the course of his statement he said:

> The detectives might well say that it is an affair for a Sherlock Holmes to investigate. Curiously enough I have received a communication from Sir Arthur Conan Doyle, who is a distant relative of mine, asking if he could give any advice. I don't know whether my family jewels will ever be found, but my own opinion is that whoever has got the Crown Jewels will find that he has got a white elephant, for I have sufficient faith in the rarity and the beauty of the stones to feel that they cannot change hands without detection. Whoever has got them, the best thing they can do is to return them by parcel post and get the reward.

Meanwhile Sergeant Sheehan had left for England. Whether the Irish police found difficulty in unravelling the intricacies of the English railway time-tables, or whether they had devised this subtle plot to catch Mr Hodgson unawares, even perhaps when he was wearing the royal diamonds, Sheehan presented himself at Abbey Cottage, Alnwick, a day earlier than Mr Hodgson had been told to expect him.

So completely removed from the usual peaceful tenor of his life was this visit from the police that, on the evening of 17th July, Hodgson wrote an account of it to Mr Chamney, the friend who had introduced him to Vicars.

'As I shall be more or less either from home or busily engaged for the next fortnight,' (he wrote) 'I think I must tonight tell you of my being interviewed by the Dublin detective. His name is Shehan [*sic*] and his rank a sergeant of police. It was intimated to me that he would call on me today but he arrived yesterday, so I have been interviewed at great length on both days. The officer turned me inside out and, although he looked a jolly fellow, was close-mouthed and did not even inform me of the state of the weather in Dublin. I chaffed him that he intended to have promotion out of the job!

'I replied to the long list of questions which he had brought with him, candidly and fully, and finally signed the deposition which he drew up from my evidence. He made one request which I thought unusual & refused, viz. to be allowed to peruse the letters which I had received from Sir Arthur Vicars since the discovery of the robbery. On reflection I stated that, if he could obtain from Sir Arthur a letter or telegram addressed to me authorising me to produce the letters, I would be ready to do so.

'In the event this was done and this afternoon, after receiving a telegram[1] purporting to come from Sir Arthur, I not only produced the telegram and two letters, received from Sir Arthur since the robbery was discovered, but permitted him to copy them. What was the officer's object I cannot even guess, but I have written to Sir Arthur to inform him of what I have done.

'I could almost fancy he would like to have found traces of the Jewels and to have taken me back with him a captive bound to his chariot wheels. . . .'

One detail in Mr Hodgson's statement probably puzzled Sergeant Sheehan. It appeared that, when Vicars offered to show him the insignia, Hodgson exhibited very little interest. He was much more anxious to examine an object displayed in the glass case in the strong-room. This was a Garter, embroided with the motto HONI SOIT QUI MAL Y PENSE, said to have belonged to the great Duke of Marlborough. Although Vicars permitted his visitor to handle this ducal relic, he insisted upon producing the Crown Jewels from the safe.

About the time Sergeant Sheehan arrived in Alnwick, Vicars received a message which served to strengthen still more his resurgent hopes. The Irish International Exhibition was, like every other project of its kind, a magnet for every sort of charlatan, rogue and adventurer who hoped to find among the crowd of visitors enough credulous people to fill their yawning pockets. To any of these the offered reward of £1,000 would be of immediate interest; but it was not easy, short of knowing where the missing Jewels were, to see how the theft might be turned to

---

[1] This telegram is preserved with Mr Chamney's other papers relative to the case in the Genealogical Office. It reads: 'I have no objection to your shewing my letters to Dublin police officer now in Alnwick, Ulster.'

their own profit and advantage. One woman, however, working in the Italian section of the exhibition, decided that she would get in touch with Vicars. She wrote to tell him that her daughter had had a vision concerning the stolen insignia.

On receipt of this message Vicars sought Shackleton's help. Not only would it be scarcely fitting for a King of Arms to embark upon so dubious a mission himself; but Vicars always regarded Shackleton as, above everything else, a man whose experience and gifts enabled him to establish good relations with members of every circle of society. Shackleton, for whom each day dawned as a period holding opportunities for both profit and excitement, must have been delighted by the unusual nature of Vicars' request.

Whatever happened that day at Ballsbridge, Shackleton would seem to have been as impressed with the young lady's occult powers as she must have been by his good looks. Upon his return, he urged Vicars to test the visionary's gifts. So, on the following Sunday, the spiritualists of Dublin converged upon the quiet house in St James's Terrace. Earlier, in order that he might give every assistance to these unofficial seekers after the truth and the regalia, Vicars asked the police if he might exchange the safe key which he usually carried, but which was now in their custody, for the one as a rule hidden in his house. It was thought that the first of these would have the more potent influence. Rather surprisingly the authorities raised no objection to this request. Possibly, since they had discovered nothing themselves, they hoped that Vicars' unorthodox methods might give them a lead which they could follow to some purpose.

This must have been the most bizarre party which that house had ever witnessed. For one thing it will have presented to Vicars' guests so very different an appearance to the bare and hired rooms which form so often the setting for mediumistic meetings. Here, summer flowers were arranged in bowls of fine china or glittering silver, while the colourful bindings of Ulster's treasured books, the choice pieces of well-kept furniture, provided the gathering coven with glimpses of a tradition of culture which contained no place for the illogical mysteries upon which they pinned their trust.

As Vicars greeted the odd cross-section of spiritualists who had been invited to the meeting, he may well have wondered if, for once at least, Shackleton had not persuaded him to go a little too far. Presently, however, the proceedings got under way. As the curtains were drawn across the already lowered blinds, shutting away the sunlight and the trees, the familiar atmosphere of the room became charged with new and disturbing influences. The scent of the flowers diminished as the odour of spiritism increased. In spite of himself, Vicars dared to hope that he might discover something of use to him in this strange ritual.

The young woman had soon dwindled into a trance; and now, through the shadows, an unknown voice told how the missing Jewels were hidden near a tombstone which stood not far from the entrance to an old and disused churchyard in the direction of Clonsilla.

Vicars' mercurial spirits soared. It seemed to him most unlikely that the medium, a stranger to Ireland, should ever have heard of that small village with so lovely a name. He longed now for the party to end; but the medium, already coming out of her trance, must be given time to recover. Besides, Frederick Pitt was handing round the appropriate refreshments which Vicars had provided for his guests. At last, however, when the last of the initiates had gone into the sun-drenched streets, deserted now in the somnolent aftermath of Sunday dinner, Vicars and Shackleton bent together over a large-scale map of the city and the surrounding countryside.

Almost at once Ulster's hopes were touched by the frost of dismay. The oracle had been less precise than it might have been, and now it was too late to seek further clarification. There was Clonsilla: but here, lying between Dublin and that village, was the churchyard at Mulhuddart. To which of the two had that disembodied voice referred?

Nothing could be done before the morning. Vicars would have liked to drive out at once to search for the lost Jewels; but he knew that, on his voyage of discovery, he must be accompanied by at least one policeman. Otherwise, should he find the regalia, it would be so easy for the uncharitable to suggest that he himself had taken the pieces from the safe and now, unable to dispose of them, had invented this elaborate story of the *séance* to explain how the diamonds came to be in his possession.

So next morning Vicars, Peirce Mahony and Detective Sergeant Patrick Murphy drove out past Phoenix Park on their way to Mulhuddart and Clonsilla. At both places the graveyards, deserted though not closed for burials, were carefully explored. The dark nettles and white-laced cow-parsley, the rich green of the Irish grass, the long tendrils of the brambles which clutched at the men's sleeves and legs as though to engage them in conversation, were carefully probed. The curious flat-topped stones laid upon four bulbous legs, a series of macabre refectory tables, came in for special attention. The grass and weeds in the cavities below them would have served as excellent hiding-places. Sticks were poked here and there. Hope fluttered each time these struck against a stone, a discarded tin, an empty bottle, then wilted as inspection showed the obstruction to be no box of royal jewels.

As the sun rose higher in the summer sky, the three men continued, more and more despondently, to search for the lost treasure. It is unlikely that, at either place, their activities passed unnoticed. Their hopes will probably have waned to an accompaniment of impertinent questions and inspired suggestions from the gaping children and puzzled villagers who cluster about them. Despite their disappointment at finding nothing, they will all have welcomed the moment when it was clear that they must admit defeat and go home. Nevertheless it will have been a sad and silent little party who drove back towards Dublin through the flat, lush fields, dotted with whitewashed cottages and tree-girt villas spreading out to where, away on the right, the Wicklow mountains form a splendid closure to the rural scene.

Upon their arrival they will have been welcomed by Frank Shackleton, whose impending departure for England had made it impossible for him to accompany them on their quest. They will have told him and the senior police officials of their failure to discover the regalia; but both Vicars and his nephew will have come to the conclusion, during their silent drive, that this day's unfortunate activities had better be shrouded in a discreet silence.

As it was, when the findings of the Commission of Inquiry were published, no less a personage than Miss Marie Corelli, the celebrated novelist, seized upon this incident and fashioned it into a whip with which to castigate the unfortunate Vicars. Writing in *London Opinion* she declared:

> Nothing more distressingly comical has ever happened than the introduction of official dealings with 'clairvoyance' into a Parliamentary Blue Book. It will be something for future historians to make game of. . . .
>
> As for Sir Arthur Vicars, he must have been what is called 'a figure of fun'. Indeed groping about for the Jewels in two cemeteries at the behest of a 'Clairvoyante!' If there is anything to be specially quoted against him beyond his evident carelessness, it is this outrageous display of utter stupidity, which has certainly exposed him completely to popular contempt. For the bulk of the British people are still sane and healthy, and can see through a thing or two. They are wide awake to the fact that while God is blasphemed in the press and Christ 'preached down' in many pulpits, the 'upper' classes are giving themselves over to such superstitious observances as degraded even the paganism of a barbarous age. They view with unutterable scorn men who, placed in positions of trust under Government, are found dabbling with conjuring tricks of 'clairvoyant' humbug. . . .

CHAPTER TWO

1

It is difficult to trace the exact sequence of faltering steps by which the Irish detectives pursued their quarry. On July 18th, however, following perhaps the arrival of Sergeant Sheehan's report on his activities at Alnwick, Sergeant Murphy obtained a second signed statement from Vicars. Although there was little in this that was new, one or two points are worthy of notice.

'For the last few years it was my custom,' explained Vicars, 'on occasions of full dress nights, when the Jewels were worn, to detach my safe key from my private bunch at my residence and put it in the tail pocket of my tunic. The bunch I then left in my uniform overcoat pocket, and also the office door key loose.

'Since Mr Narramore[1] left the Castle I have always hung my uniform overcoat behind the door of His Excellency's Private Secretary's[2] room. Prior to that I always left my uniform overcoat hanging in Mr Narramore's room. . . . The key of the strong room door, on those nights, I always left on my watch-chain, with any money, etc., in my dressing-table drawer, duly locked, the key of which was on my bunch. . . .

'I can give no reason for giving Stivey the safe key on 6th July, beyond the fact that I was for the moment engaged with a letter, and the collar and case I wished him to carry down. At any rate I followed Stivey down, and when I entered the library Stivey had not even opened the safe. My recollection is that he was in a stooped position at it, having just ascertained that the safe was unlocked. . . .

'The spare key of the strong room is kept concealed in one of the drawers at the very back, wrapt in paper. This is the key that Mr Burtchaell gave up some time ago. . . . Stivey and I were the only persons, so far as I know, who knew that the spare key of the strong room was concealed in the drawer there.'

[1] ? Head of the Catering Department.
[2] Lord Herschell.

This does leave one with the impression that anyone who knew Vicars intimately could have obtained impressions of all the keys, even perhaps the keys themselves, if they had wished to do so.

No one seems ever to have viewed Stivey with any real suspicion. Perhaps he was either too palpably honest or too patently stupid to be suspected seriously. In any case the eyes of the police were soon to be directed elsewhere.

Upon his return to England, Shackleton was not displeased to find that he was in even greater demand than usual. Then, as now, there were many in Society, or existing hopefully upon its perimeter, who discovered an especial pleasure in suggesting that, where matters of public interest or the private behaviour of others were concerned, they were in the enviable position of knowing rather more than did most other people. Which is why, at this time, those of his friends who were still in London were delighted to receive from Shackleton his account of the robbery; and, in return, he polished his story so that it would, almost inevitably, set any Edwardian table in a roar.

Lord Ronald Gower was charmed with his young friend's recital. The description of the *séance* and the subsequent search among the lichen-covered tombstones held for him a quality, at once horrific and absurd, which suited well with his somewhat Romantic Gothic taste. But he had no wish to keep to himself so pungent a comment on the contemporary scene. He knew that his niece, Lady Mary Glyn, was particularly interested in Irish affairs at that time. Her husband, the Bishop of Peterborough, had at one time been chaplain to the Aberdeens; and the latter had continued to take a kindly interest in the young Glyns. The Bishop's son was one of the Lord Lieutenant's A.D.C.s, and his two daughters had spent the Dublin Season as guests at Viceregal Lodge. So, when Lord Ronald was invited to spend a few days at the episcopal palace at Peterborough, he thought he would be doing the Glyns a kindness if he suggested that Dublin Herald might also be asked at the same time. Besides, Shackleton had already met Lady Mary's brother, the Duke of Argyll. In consequence, on July 31st 1907,

Frank Shackleton signed his name in the leather-bound visitors' book which still preserves for us the ebb and flow of the Glyns' guests.

Although it must have been rarely that Dublin Herald moved in clerical society, that he did so now is of interest only because its sequel throws a revealing light upon his character.

He came to Peterborough as a stranger, a friend of his hostess's uncle and, after he left, it is doubtful whether he ever saw any of the Glyns again. Yet, when he found it necessary to protest his respectability, he was to cite his friendship with the Duke of Argyll and the Bishop of Peterborough as evidence of his established probity. One is left with the feeling that, despite his social successes, his flat in Park Lane, his membership of four London clubs and his appointment in the Office of Arms, his real friends were not such as would inspire immediate confidence among either the police or the general public.

During those summer days Shackleton moved about a good deal. He spent some time at the Crown Hotel in Harrogate. He visited Bembridge in the Isle of Wight and, whenever he could, he went down to Devonshire. Not only was his brother Ernest there, preparing for his voyage to the Antarctic, but Frank was able to run over to see a friend of his in Tavistock. This was a Miss Mary Josephine Browne, a lady of mature years who seems by nature to have been a universal aunt. She had long been a friend of Frank Hird, who had taken Lord Ronald Gower down to Devonshire to see her on their first visit together to Britain and, later, she had been one of the first guests invited to stay at Hammerfield. It must have been through Frank Hird that Shackleton was first introduced to the chatelaine of Osborne Villa, but Miss Browne very soon capitulated to his charm. It was not long before she came to believe that her relationship with Shackleton was 'akin to that of mother and son'.

While Dublin Herald followed this round of social pleasures, Vicars found it increasingly difficult to forget the appalling catastrophe which had befallen him. Yet his colleagues at the Castle proved very sympathetic and his relations with the Lord-Lieutenant remained as cordial as ever. At the same time, however, he could not enter the library in the Bedford Tower without seeing the empty and now useless safe. There were, too, other constant reminders of his loss: such, for instance, as the visit he received from his friend Mr McEnnery, junior. (It will be remembered that this gentleman had spent one night early in July at the house in St James's Terrace.) Now, a few days after Shackleton's return to England, McEnnery called on Vicars at the Office of Arms. In the course of their conversation, his visitor told Vicars that he himself was almost certain that the Jewels had been stolen by Shackleton, whom he described as a shady customer in every respect.

This statement must have been supported by a considerable weight of evidence because, although till now Vicars had repudiated any suggestion that one of his staff might be responsible for the theft, from this time on he viewed Shackleton with ever-increasing suspicion. Thus it is much to be regretted that, although McEnnery was questioned by the police about his conversation with Vicars, and the statement he made to them taken to the Court of Inquiry, the Commissioners decided that there was no reason why its contents should be made public. So when, in August, Goldney came to stay with Vicars for the Dublin Horse Show, he found that a very unexpected change had taken place in his host's attitude towards Shackleton; and the stories he was able to tell of that young man's curious methods regarding money were seized upon by Vicars as additional proof that his suspicions were well-founded.

On his arrival in Dublin, Goldney found Vicars suffering from delayed shock and the continuing strain of the police inquiries. He decided, therefore, that he must persuade him to go away for a time; he must come to Abbots Barton and find there renewed health and peace of mind. Vicars accepted the invitation but, despite the change of air, he found it impossible to forget what had happened. The two antiquarians, King of Arms and Mayor of Canterbury, found small comfort in their mutual interests. Again and again their talk would return to the subject of Frank Shackleton and all he might have done.

2

At this juncture Shackleton became the victim of an extraordinary sequence of events which, but for the exemplary fair-
ness displayed by the police, might have had disastrous consequences for him.

The first of these incidents took place while he was staying
at Harrogate. A fellow guest at the Crown Hotel there was Sir
Patrick Coll, a former Law Officer of the Crown. Speaking to
Shackleton one day, he mentioned that he had seen a report in
a newspaper to the effect that the Crown Jewels had been recovered. Understandably surprised and hurt that no one in the
Office of Arms had thought to inform him of this development,
Shackleton wrote to Vicars and to Peirce Mahony asking why
he had not been told.

Before he received any reply to these letters, Shackleton had
to meet Goldney to discuss certain financial matters. In the
course of a somewhat uncomfortable interview, Shackleton
finally countered the other's bitter complaints by demanding,
'Why didn't you tell me the Jewels were recovered?'

Goldney was now as surprised as his companion had been
when Sir Patrick Coll had spoken to him. It is clear that
Shackleton must have written to Vicars in Dublin and the letter
had not reached Abbots Barton before Goldney came to London for this meeting. Goldney told Shackleton that he had
heard nothing about this; but the younger man assured him
that he had heard the news on very good authority.

The more Goldney considered this new development, the
more he felt convinced that it was part of some deep-laid scheme
of Shackleton's. So, before returning to Canterbury, he hurried
round to Scotland Yard and asked to see Chief Inspector Kane.

This officer, still smarting under a sense of grievance at the
treatment he had received from the authorities at Dublin,
exhibited no enthusiasm when Goldney was shown into his
office. He listened to his visitor's story of the interview he had
just had with Shackleton and, at the end, was forced to admit
that it was all very curious. He was, however, convinced that the
careful checks the police had carried out to test Shackleton's
movements between 11th June and 9th July had proved beyond
all doubt that Dublin Herald had not been in Ireland between

those dates. But he promised Goldney that he would make inquiries about this report that the Jewels had been found. That, he told his visitor, was completely untrue.

Eventually Goldney left Scotland Yard and, as the train carried him back through the summer evening towards Canterbury, he felt more and more convinced that, by going to see Kane, he had taken a decisive step towards bringing the handsome and dangerous Shackleton to justice. And that evening, as he and Vicars strolled together in the bell-haunted twilight from one tall monkey-puzzle to another, he found reassurance as Ulster, listening to his story, assured him that he had done the wisest, in fact the only, thing.

Meanwhile Shackleton returned to Harrogate. There he found a letter from Peirce Mahony telling him that the report that the Jewels had been returned had appeared in a newspaper but had been entirely without foundation. So far as he knew, the police were as far as ever from recovering the diamonds.

Within the next day or two Shackleton's aggrieved letter reached Vicars at Abbots Barton. He thereupon wrote to his former friend and confidant. After touching upon the financial matters which were causing Goldney so much anxiety, Vicars continued:

'Now that you evidently know the whereabouts of the Jewels, from what you have said to both Frank and me, I hope you have told Mr Kane everything calculated to facilitate matters.'

Scarcely can Shackleton have recovered from this undeserved slap than he became involved in a still more extraordinary misunderstanding.

On 28th August, while Vicars was still at Abbots Barton, a telegram addressed to Lord Aberdeen arrived in Dublin. This, which bore no signature, contained a succinct but startling message: '*Jewels are in box, 9, Hadley Street, Dublin.*'

Sir James Dougherty was instructed to send a cipher telegram to the Home Secretary asking that he might be sent the original of this message. To this application by the Home Office the Secretary of the General Post Office was not forthcoming. He said – which had been clearly understood from the beginning – that the telegram had been handed in at either Malvern or Great Malvern. Upon 30th August, having heard nothing from London, Dougherty telegraphed once more. An Assistant Under-Secretary replied that a cipher telegram was being sent immediately. The Home Secretary[1] now signed a warrant authorising the Post Office to search for, and to produce, the mysterious telegraph form. When this was found and sent to the Home Office, it was accompanied by a note which stated that, since it was the addressee who wished to see the original, no warrant had been necessary. . . .

The first arrival of this telegram had brought a new resurgence of hope to the authorities at Dublin. All too soon, however, this was shattered. The police, instructed to surround and search the house with all speed and secrecy, found themselves unable to carry out these orders. There was no Hadley Street in Dublin.

Not yet, however, would the authorities accept defeat. The telegram had been sent, so someone must have had a purpose in composing and paying for it. That person must be found. The original form was sent to Kane at Scotland Yard. After the handwriting had been compared with other specimens in Kane's files, that officer called on Shackleton, who was then in London, and asked him if he would go to Scotland Yard as he had something to show him. Dublin Herald at once accompanied Kane to the Yard, where the Chief Inspector produced the original of the mysterious telegram. Folding this so that no more than the word 'Dublin' was visible, he held it out for Shackleton's inspection.

'Whose writing is that?' he demanded.

Acting upon the meagre evidence afforded by that isolated word, Shackleton said that it was his. Thereupon Kane opened the form and laid it in front of the bewildered herald, who found himself reading a message he had never seen before. Up till now Kane had paid little attention to the accusations made against Shackleton by Vicars and Goldney; but now, listening to the young man's protestations, he felt considerable doubts. After all, it must be a singularly stupid person who cannot recognise his own handwriting.

---

[1] Herbert Gladstone (1854–1930); Home Secretary 1905–9; created Viscount Gladstone and appointed 1st Governor General of South Africa, 1909.

Dismissing Shackleton with the injunction that he must stay in London, Kane sent an urgent message to Abbots Barton asking Vicars to come to London as soon as possible. Vicars obeyed immediately. He must have told Kane when to expect him because Shackleton was with the Chief Inspector when Ulster was shown into the office. The greetings exchanged by the two former friends were of the most glacial kind.

Shackleton had been told to say nothing. Otherwise it is impossible to believe that he could have remained silent while Kane repeated the tragic pantomime of their earlier interview. The detective folded the telegram so that only the word 'Dublin' was visible. Then he handed it to Vicars.

'Whose writing is that?' he asked.

Vicars studied the paper carefully. Then he turned to look at Shackleton.

'I suppose you did.'

A long silence followed. So far as we know, Shackleton made no attempt to deny, to argue or to explain. Kane was the first to move. He put down the telegraph form without allowing Vicars to see the remainder of the message.

Vicars left at once. Shackleton remained a little longer. Probably Kane tried to persuade him to admit that he had sent the telegram. Then Shackleton left. He went out into the crowded, sunlit streets with two thoughts uppermost in his mind. He knew that his friendship with Vicars was at an end; and he believed he might be arrested at any moment on a charge of having played some part in the theft of the Crown Jewels. Going to his club he wrote a letter to his brother Ernest. Then, fearing that time was running out, he arranged for a district messenger to take it down to Devonshire at once.

3

Kane at once reported to the authorities at Dublin all that had happened in connection with the telegram. At the same time, shaken in his belief that Shackleton had had no part in the theft, he reopened his inquiries into the young man's movements since he returned to England from Ireland in June. In the end he was more than ever certain that Shackleton could have played no active part in the disappearance of the Jewels. Why, then, had he sent that telegram?

A week later, on 4th September, a second telegram from Great Malvern was received by the Lord Lieutenant. This one, however, bore the signature of the sender, Mr Bullock Webster. The police questioning which ensued uncovered a very odd story.

A great deal of tedious research among local records of the period has failed to produce any information regarding the Bullock Websters although, at the Commission of Inquiry, it was stated that Mr Bullock Webster was a gentleman of high repute in Great Malvern. We have therefore been drawn to the conclusion that the Bullock Websters were probably people of some means, staying in one of the hotels and seeking benefit from the Malvern waters. What is certain is that the police found the first telegram had been sent in consequence of a dream in which, so Mrs Webster believed, the whereabouts of the regalia had been revealed to her. That the name of the sender was not given suggests that Mr Webster regarded the whole matter with considerable dubiety.

But nothing happened. Scan the newspapers as they would, the Websters could find nothing regarding the recovery of the Crown Jewels.

After a week had gone past Mr Bullock Webster again went to the post office, but this time appended his name and address to the message.

When, after the publication of the report of the Commission of Inquiry, Miss Marie Corelli attacked Vicars for holding the *séance* at his house, she also poured scorn on poor Mrs Bullock Webster. That Miss Corelli had failed to understand much of all she read in the Report will have made her criticisms of Mrs Webster no easier for that lady to bear.

> It will be something [wrote Miss Corelli] for future historians to make game of when they read how no less a person than the Dublin Herald, Mr Shackleton, listened to the innocent babblings of the wife of 'a gentleman of high repute' respecting a vision wherein the Jewels were stated to be in a box at No. 9 Hadley Street, Dublin. Poor Mr Shackleton! It was really very funny of him. Perhaps if the visionary had been the wife of a gentleman of less repute, no attention would have

been paid to her statement. Friends of the humbler class will note by this how good a thing it is, my brethren, to be of 'high repute'. You can do everything then. You can dream dreams, and they will actually be accepted as important facts by Government officials! Think of it! What a grand vista opens out before the dazzled eye!

Poor Mr Shackleton, indeed! It was not he who had paid attention to Mrs Bullock Webster's dreams and, although the arrival of their second telegram and Kane's subsequent interview with the Websters dispelled any continuing doubts the detective may have felt about Shackleton, that young man was being made increasingly aware that many people were beginning to view him with considerable suspicion.

While he still walked under the shadow of imminent arrest, he learned that a number of writs against himself had been presented at the house in St James's Terrace. At the same time Major Vicars, Ulster's brother, wrote to ask Shackleton if he would terminate at once the arrangement by which Ulster and he were joint tenants of the Dublin house. Major Vicars, writing at his brother's request, indicated that it would be most embarrassing to someone holding such a position as did the King of Arms to be connected with a person likely to be sued in the courts for debt.

This latest development was the result of Arthur Vicars' prolonged stay at Abbots Barton. There, amid the ill-assorted collection of antiquities with which Goldney had surrounded himself and his unprotesting mother, Ulster and Athlone Pursuivant so worked upon each other's feelings that, between them, they created a mental picture of Shackleton in the character of an arch-criminal. As a questing tongue touches again and again an aching tooth, their conversation returned always to Shackleton. Then, when imagination or spleen began to flag, they would travel up to London, together, separately or in the company of Major Vicars, and seek out Kane at Scotland Yard. There they would renew their attempts to persuade the detective that Shackleton *must* be responsible for the theft. The Chief Inspector was not impressed by their arguments. He pointed out repeatedly that no one had so far produced even a fragment of valid evidence against Dublin Herald.

This makes it all the more extraordinary that Kane, believing as he did in Shackleton's innocence, never told him that the mystery of the telegram from Great Malvern had been solved. So, as the corn in the English fields ripened towards harvest, Shackleton went in constant expectation that the police might arrest him at any moment.

CHAPTER THREE

1

Meanwhile a number of developments were taking place elsewhere.

King Edward had no intention of allowing the loss of the Irish regalia to subside into some official limbo. He wished to know what steps were being taken both to trace the thief and to recover the Jewels. Lord Aberdeen replied that the Government had offered a reward of £1,000 for information leading to the recovery of the stolen articles. As this had been announced on the day of the King's arrival in Ireland a month earlier, His Majesty was not impressed. When the succeeding weeks produced no clue but a great deal of unpleasant gossip, the King's patience grew very thin.

On 26th August, Lord Knollys, the Private Secretary, wrote to Lord Aberdeen that the King 'is not, I am afraid, satisfied with your explanation and he desires me to let you know that there is a mystery and an apparent lukewarmness about the enquiry, and in fact the whole of the proceedings, which he does not understand. He says that at the end of nearly two months, surely, if there is ever to be a clue, it must have been discovered by this time.

'His Majesty also says that somebody must have been careless in their custody of these Crown Jewels, and if so he would be glad to know, who, and whether, whoever it may be, anything in the way of punishment or reprimand has been given to him.'[1]

To the Lord Lieutenant, hoping against fading hope that, somehow or other, the police would yet discover the lost Jewels, this expression of royal disapproval came as a bitter blow. For a number of reasons Lord Aberdeen was most unwilling to follow the course indicated by Lord Knollys. He appreciated the

[1] *King Edward VII, A Biography*, by Sir Sidney Lee (Macmillan & Co., London, 1927), Vol. II, p. 473.

enthusiastic interest which Vicars brought to his work, and he felt quite sure that, should Ulster go, it would be very difficult, perhaps impossible, to find anyone else who could advise him with so much assurance upon matters of protocol and the elaborate arrangements connected with the official aspects of the viceregal court. Besides, Aberdeen was a very kindly man and he shrank from the prospect of administering to Vicars the devastating blow that would be inevitable if the King persisted in his present intention. Yet these considerations could weigh nothing at all against a direct command from the Sovereign. His melancholy eyes became more haunted still as, unavailingly, he sought a way out of his difficulties.

Then, on 17th September, when no solution of these problems had been found, Lord Knollys wrote once more. He told Lord Aberdeen that, in the King's opinion, the search for the Jewels and the thief was not being prosecuted with sufficient energy. It was His Majesty's wish that Vicars should be suspended from his office. This letter closed with a command that Lord Aberdeen should go to Balmoral on 24th September so that the King might learn more about 'this disagreeable business'.[1]

It was most unfortunate that, at this critical juncture, the Irish Secretary, Mr Birrell, should have been abroad and that, in his absence, the Lord-Lieutenant turned for advice and sympathy to the Under Secretary of State, Sir Anthony Macdonnell.[2] This rugged man of beetling shaggy brows and determined manners was of very different calibre to most of those at that time connected with the government of Ireland. The son of middle-class Irish Catholic parents, he had returned to Britain in 1902 after nearly forty years in India where, as a civil servant, he proved so able that he had held successively the appointments of Acting Chief Commissioner in Burma, Chief Commissioner of the Central Provinces, Acting Lieutenant-Governor of Bengal and Lieutenant-Governor of the N.W. Provinces. While awaiting a new appointment, he was invited by George Wyndham[3] to assist in carrying through his programme of Land Reform in Ireland.

[1] King Edward VII, A Biography, by Sir Sidney Lee (Macmillan & Co., London, 1927), Vol. II, p. 474.
[2] (1844–1925); created Baron Macdonnell of Swinford, co. Mayo, July, 1908.
[3] (1863–1913); Secretary of State for Ireland, 1900–5.

Macdonnell possessed unrivalled experience in settling agrarian problems among hostile races and classes; and, although the post he was now offered as Under Secretary of State appeared much less important than those he had held in India, it carried with it a position of independent influence over administration and an authority far beyond those normally associated with an Under Secretary. Unfortunately his long experience in Asia was scarcely applicable to Ireland where, despite his success as an administrator, his methods antagonised the easy-going Irish Civil Service and aroused the hostility of the Unionists. Oddly enough, as will be seen, Macdonnell's advice to Lord Aberdeen on this occasion savoured more of devious oriental diplomacy than the uncompromising directness usually associated with him.

During the days of anxious waiting while the Lord-Lieutenant prepared for his visit to Balmoral, no decisions were taken and no clues to the mystery were found. After more than two months the police had discovered nothing.

2

Meanwhile Vicars was planning to return to Ireland. Before leaving Abbots Barton for the last time, he went with Goldney to Scotland Yard in the hope of finally persuading Kane that Shackleton must be primarily responsible for the disappearance of the Jewels. In this they were unsuccessful but, on his arrival in Dublin, Vicars lost no time before repeating his accusations to the Irish detectives.

He first broached the subject to Sergeant Sheehan, asking him to search the house in St James's Terrace, where he thought Shackleton might have hidden the regalia. Sheehan's search proved unavailing. Then, on 19th September, Vicars propounded a new theory. He was in the hall of the Office of Arms with Kerr when he suddenly pointed to the door leading to the cellar.

'If that door had been locked,' he said, 'it would never have happened.'

He vouchsafed no further explanation and Kerr asked no questions. Possibly the detective thought that Vicars was suggesting he had not carried out his nightly search of the premises as thoroughly as he had claimed. Then, after a pause that was more abortive than pregnant, Vicars spoke again, using that oddly oracular style we associate with Chief Inspector Kane.

'They [the Jewels] were taken by a man you know well,' he declared. 'He was a guest in my house and he treacherously took impressions of my keys when I was in my bath. He often came to this office for his letters on Sunday, and he used my latchkey to get in. He is in Paris at this moment, and here is a cipher telegram that I am after receiving about him. They are now a white elephant in his hands and they will be returned.'

(Maddeningly, this cipher telegram is mentioned nowhere else in the printed records, and no one seems ever to have made inquiries about it. The sender was almost certainly Goldney, who was never averse to leaving his mother at Abbots Barton while he visited Paris. Also, since he is remembered in Canterbury as walking the streets in a long black cloak lined with scarlet, the role of private detective shadowing Shackleton in order to establish his guilt would have come easily enough.)

As Kerr remained silent, Vicars repeated his theory about the door of the cellar. He said he believed the theft had taken place on Sunday, 30th June; but when he suggested that someone had entered the Office that day and hidden in the basement, Kerr told him brusquely that the idea was ridiculous. He had himself searched the building that night from top to bottom. Then the detective turned to Vicars with a respectful inquiry.

'Cannot it be definitely fixed whether that gentleman was in Ireland on that Sunday?'

'He could be in Ireland,' answered Vicars. 'He could be in Dublin and nothing known about it. Could not he have been staying on the North Wall?'

However many theories might be examined and demolished, Vicars could always think up another. Kane must have told him that he and his men had checked and re-checked Shackleton's movements for the periods he claimed to have been in England and that they were satisfied that Dublin Herald could not have come over to Ireland during that time. But because this would invalidate Vicars' latest theory, he refused to accept it.

I *The Bedford Tower, Dublin Castle.*
In 1907 the Office of Arms, now the Genealogical Office.

II *Sir Arthur Vicars*, K.C.V.O., *Ulster King of Arms.*
From the portrait by an unknown artist, now in the Genealogical Office.

III *Carriages arriving for a Drawing Room at Dublin Castle, 1908.*
From the painting by Rose Barton in the collection of Dr Michael Magan.

IV *Mrs Mary Farrell.*

V *The Insignia of the Order of St Patrick.*

Top left: *The Collar worn by a Knight of St Patrick.*
Top right: *The Badge.*
Bottom: *The Star.*

F. BENNETT-GOLDNEY,
The Popular Candidate.

VI *Francis Bennett-Goldney, Mayor of Canterbury.*
From a postcard issued during one of his parliamentary election campaigns.

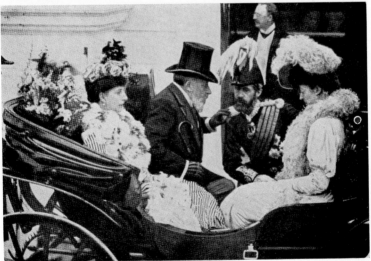

VII Top: *Kilmorna House, County Kerry.*

Bottom: *Lord Aberdeen bids farewell to King Edward* VII, *Queen Alexandra and the Princess Victoria at the end of the royal visit to the Irish International Exhibition, July, 1907.*

VIII *Ichabod! – Kilmorna as it is today.*

3

It would be interesting to know what passed between King Edward and Lord Aberdeen when they met amid the tartan splendours of Balmoral. The King, the owner of the lost property, must have been even more impressive than usual; while the Lord-Lieutenant must have resembled nothing so much as a Highland shepherd forced to tell the laird that the best of his flock had been stolen away.

If Lord Aberdeen had gone to that meeting in the hope that no drastic steps would be taken, and the veil of discretion drawn over the whole unfortunate incident, he soon realised that so comfortable a solution could not be expected. If he had not been told earlier, he must have learnt now that King Edward was determined that one name above all must be shielded from the slightest breath of scandal. Having accepted this new and startling development, Lord Aberdeen played his hand with considerable skill. He persuaded the King that no further action should be taken for a fortnight. Not that Lord Aberdeen can have supposed that this brief respite would produce the Jewels; but like many people he believed, in the face of years of experience to the contrary, that the worst never happens. Besides, he had discussed the matter with Macdonnell, whom he regarded as a thoroughly reliable man. The Lord-Lieutenant derived real comfort from the knowledge that Macdonnell had 'decided that the best way of treating the matter would be to get rid of Vicars on some other pretext'.[1]

His complacency was a good deal shaken, however, when he returned to Dublin and discovered that Macdonnell's plan was to make Vicars' position so uncomfortable that he would be forced to resign. With this in view, he had seen that a calculated, seemingly casual word was dropped here and there to the effect that Scotland Yard knew there was a connection between Vicars and a group of homosexuals in London. That was enough, and the damage was done. The drawing-rooms and clubs of Dublin proved no less prone to the dissemination of scandal and rumour than had the crowded bazaars of those of the King's

---

[1] *My Diaries*, by Wilfrid Scawen Blunt (Martin Secker, London), Vol. II, p. 192.

eastern dominions over which Macdonnell had at one time
ruled.

The seed of calumny grew swiftly. The drink parties which
Vicars had given from time to time at the Office of Arms were
now remembered with suspicion and surmise, for it was remembered that these were always exclusively male. No one bothered
to think that Vicars' guests had been drawn almost entirely from
others who, like himself, worked in the Castle and were delighted with this most agreeable innovation devised by Ulster,
a drink and relaxed conversation before returning home to
dinner. It was also remembered, to Vicars' despite, that the
Board of Works had stipulated that he must on no account be
allowed to live in the Bedford Tower. There must have been
some good reason for that. . . .

Macdonnell now drew up a report which was based on a
curious admixture of the rumours he had himself inspired and
the accretions these had gathered on their way through Dublin
society; and, reading it, Lord Aberdeen realised that nothing
was more likely to drag into the open just such a scandal as the
King was most anxious to avoid.

For King Edward was actuated now by considerations which
had little or nothing to do with the Crown Jewels. He was intent
only upon preventing the Press and the public from learning
that his brother-in-law, the Duke of Argyll, had been on terms
of friendship, however slight, with a man, Shackleton, who had
been an associate of that clique of influential homosexuals.

Only a few months earlier, European Society had watched in
bewilderment the extraordinary series of events which culminated in the departure from the German Court of the Prince von
Eulenberg-Hertefeld, the Kaiser's favourite. At the same time
three of the Imperial A.D.C.s had been dismissed – and two of
these had been sons of Prince Albrecht of Prussia – as well as
the Commandant of Berlin and the Master of Ceremonies, both
of whom were relieved of their posts. All had been accused of
homosexual activities; and, of the succeeding trials and law-
suits which followed, King Edward had declared that not even
the Hohenzollerns had behaved as stupidly as this before. Knowing all this, Lord Aberdeen could do nothing but forward the
report on Vicars and hope for the best.

At the end of the two weeks of grace Lord Knollys wrote

again to the Lord-Lieutenant, telling him that His Majesty's wishes must now be carried out. So, on 12th October, the juggernaut of royal displeasure crushed first the humblest member of the staff at the Office of Arms. We do not know what reason was given; but Stivey was dismissed and retired to spend his declining years amid the cold and sober comforts of the Wesleyan Soldiers' Home at Newbridge, County Kildare.

Not until 23rd October did Lord Aberdeen translate into action the orders he had received. On that day, in a letter to Vicars, Sir James Dougherty wrote that 'His Majesty had come to the conclusion that he would reconstitute this office, and that his services were no longer in regard'.

A few days later Lord Aberdeen wrote to inform the King that his orders had been obeyed, and that Ulster, Shackleton, Mahony and Bennett-Goldney had all been asked to resign. This is not true of Vicars who, as we have seen, had been summarily dismissed. It is doubtful whether it was true as regards Peirce Mahony. But no doubt the Lord-Lieutenant wished to placate the King.

These dismissals would not appear so harsh if similar steps had been taken with those responsible for the efficiency of the military and police guards at Dublin Castle. Neither the Commissioners of Police nor the officer commanding the military garrison were ever interrogated, much less dismissed or asked to resign. There seems little reasonable doubt that the King's actions at this time were dictated by his urgent anxiety lest the Duke of Argyll's reputation might be smirched by gossip. With that excess of righteous indignation which confirmed practitioners of natural vice display so often when unnatural vice is under discussion, King Edward could not wait to find out whether there was any truth in the suppositions which had been put forward by the police at Scotland Yard. Vicars must go immediately; but there must be no scandal, no risk of legal action.

And all the time, in Dublin, the volume of rumour was growing. It was odd how much conversation could spring from what were then usually described as 'unmentionable crimes'. When Shackleton, deprived of his post as Dublin Herald and ostracised by Vicars, found himself fighting for his social survival, he did not hesitate to use those inspired rumours for his own ends.

As Vicars was to write to his friend Mr Fuller, the official architect to the Church of Ireland:

> Shackleton, when he was suspected, worked the alleged scandal for all he was worth & even blackened his own character! threatening to produce a social scandal & involve high persons.[1]

[1] It is difficult to trace the exact sequence of events. We are inclined to believe that Shackleton's name did not appear in the report on homosexuals drawn up at Scotland Yard, though it is almost certain that he was the link between these men and Vicars. It seems more probable that he was the subject of a later police investigation, possibly undertaken at the request of the King, and that it was as a result of this that Birrell referred to Shackleton as 'an abandoned ruffian' (see p. 150).

BOOK THREE

The Interlude

CHAPTER ONE

1

If the King and Lord-Lieutenant hoped that the steps they had taken would settle the matter once and for all, they were to be vastly disappointed. For whatever his colleagues might decide to do, Vicars had no intention of resigning or accepting the royal dismissal.

Upon the receipt of Dougherty's letter, Ulster wrote directly to the King, petitioning His Majesty to look into the matter personally. Considering that the decision to remove Vicars and his staff from their posts had been taken by the King alone, following the advice of no one, there is something rather distasteful about the answer he returned to Vicars' request. Lord Knollys wrote that Ulster's appeal must be made to the official authorities. . . .

In acknowledging the receipt of Dougherty's letter, Vicars asked that a full inquiry into all the circumstances connected with the theft of the insignia might be held. Two days later, on 25th October, Dougherty replied that 'His Excellency is advised that your office has been legally and properly terminated, and I am, therefore, to inform you that your request for an inquiry cannot be complied with'.

One by one the doors were being closed upon him; but Vicars refused to accept these repeated denials. On the day that he received Dougherty's letter, he wrote to him once more:

'I would remind you that I have held the office of Ulster King of Arms since January, 1893. During that time I have served under the following Lords Lieutenant: Lord Crewe, Lord Cadogan and Lord Dudley, none of whom has ever found fault with the manner in which I discharged my duties. On the contrary, I have received high praise from them, as well as from H.R.H. the Prince of Wales and H.R.H. the Duke of Connaught.' He then repeated his request that an official inquiry should be held.

Shocked and flustered by this unexpected obstinacy, Lord Aberdeen sought the advice of Augustine Birrell, who had now returned from his holiday on the Continent. He did not approve of the advice given by Macdonnell but, since the latter had now himself gone on holiday, Birrell was reluctant to alter decisions already taken. He suggested, however, that Vicars should be seen by Lord Aberdeen and himself. The meeting, which took place on 28th October, achieved nothing, except that Birrell read from a typed document what Vicars was to describe as 'trivial charges of negligence, some of which were totally incorrect'. It was into the ensuing period of deadlock, with Vicars repeatedly demanding the inquiry which the authorities had decided must not take place, that his stepbrother, Peirce O'Mahony, returned to Ireland from Bulgaria.

It will be remembered that for two years, ever since Vicars had appointed O'Mahony's son to the post of Cork Herald, the two stepbrothers had ceased to communicate with one another. But the treatment meted out to Vicars, of which Peirce had been kept advised by his elder brother George, brought him to Ulster's aid and support. 'From that day to this,' he wrote later of his return to Ireland in 1907, 'I have never ceased to work for the vindication of my brother's character.' Throughout his long and colourful career this bonny fighter worked to help those he judged little able to help themselves.

While still at Magdalen College, Oxford, in 1870, as a young man of twenty, Peirce O'Mahony joined with another Protestant undergraduate to found a Home Rule Club in the University. Then, after serving for several years as an Assistant Land Commissioner in Ireland, he stood for Parliament and was elected member for North Meath, a seat he held from 1886 to 1890. In that year, when the controversy over Parnell's leadership split the Nationalist Party into two fiercely opposed factions, O'Mahony declared himself wholeheartedly for Parnell. When, at the general election, he was opposed by Michael Davitt, the leader of the anti-Parnellites, the contest was fought with a bitterness rarely equalled even in Irish politics. Davitt was elected but unseated on petition. He refused to face O'Mahony a second time and withdrew, his place being taken by James Gibney who was finally declared the victor by 258 votes.

O'Mahony retired to Kilmorna and was reading for the Bar

when, in 1900, he inherited the estate of Grange Con from an uncle, a fact which decided him not to take his call. Between that time and 1907 he paid two visits to Russia, where he laid claim to, and eventually won, the great fortune amassed by his ancestor, Peirce Lacy, a Jacobite exile who became a general in the service of Catherine the Great. (Presumably George Mahony had relinquished his claim to his younger and more active brother.) While in Russia, Peirce discovered a new cause to champion, the aspirations of the Bulgarians to gain their independence from the Turks. Until recently, if not now, a street in Sofia bore his name in commemoration of the part he had played in their struggle for freedom. Not only did he found an orphanage in Macedonia for Bulgar refugees, but he also brought a number to Ireland, educating them at Trinity College, Dublin, where he insisted that a chaplain of the Greek Orthodox Church should be installed. Later, he became a convert to that faith.

In 1912 he succeeded to the title of The O'Mahony of Kerry; and throughout the 1914–18 War he co-operated with John Redmond in supporting the policies of the British Government. For his services this determined Nationalist was created a Commander of the British Empire. By 1927, the year in which his second son was elected to the Dáil, The O'Mahony was age-ing but still game for a fight.

Although an adherent of the Orthodox Church, he had con-tinued to receive, when at Grange Con, Communion according to the Anglican rite. At this point, however, the accommodating rector died and was succeeded by one who refused to administer the sacraments to a member of a church not in communion with the Church of Ireland. In the ensuing battle, fought by The O'Mahony with all his old determination, the rector won. Peirce, however, had no intention of passing his declining years without the consolations of religion; and, since there was no longer a chaplain of the Orthodox Church at Trinity College, he turned to the Catholic Church and was received into its sustaining arms. In 1930, The O'Mahony of Kerry, a true descendant in fact and in spirit of the Wild Geese, passed to glory. Such was the man who now espoused Vicars' cause; and there can never have been any doubt that, henceforward, there would be plenty of action.

8

His first move was to approach John Redmond, the leader of the Parliamentary Irish Party, to enlist the support of the Irish members in the House of Commons. This cannot have been an easy step for him to take because, only in the previous May, the two men had been at variance. Shortly before the Irish Convention was to meet to decide upon the attitude of the Parliamentary Party to Birrell's adulterated version of the Home Rule measures so long promised by the Liberals, O'Mahony had written to Redmond urging him to permit five members, debarred for one reason or another from the Convention, to attend the meeting. Among these five were Timothy Healy and William O'Brien. The latter's paper, *Irish People*, described Redmond's answer to this appeal as 'so curt and contemptuous that it is hardly distinguishable from an open insult'. Healy, a bitter opponent of Parnell, had not seen O'Mahony for seventeen years but he now published a letter thanking him for his initiative and stressing that it had been taken without his knowledge.

Now, in October, Peirce wrote once more to Redmond. He received a reply which, too optimistically, he construed as a promise of help. A meeting between them was arranged but it was not a success. O'Mahony seems to have forgotten how often and bitterly the Nationalists had complained that Redmond was altogether too friendly with Birrell. At last, however, he realised that Redmond had discussed Vicars' case with the Irish Secretary and had no intention of helping either Ulster or O'Mahony. To his continuing appeals Redmond returned cold and reserved answers. Finally the latter told O'Mahony that Birrell had indicated quite plainly that a charge of a grave character lay behind the accusation of carelessness brought against Vicars. Redmond would say no more, except that he could not recommend the Parliamentary Party to support his cause.

Shocked and angry, unable to break through the web of Redmond's ambiguities, O'Mahony left to seek an interview with Birrell. When they met, on November 2nd, he at once demanded to know what were the true charges levelled against his brother. When Birrell explained that 'the grave charge' was that Vicars 'had associated with a man of undesirable character', O'Mahony requested formally that a public inquiry might be held.   Birrell was suavely sympathetic. He admitted that, if

Vicars and his friends pressed for an inquiry, one must be held; but he pointed out that, in such a case, where questions of character were involved, even the innocent might be besmirched. But O'Mahony was not to be persuaded. He realised at once that Birrell was referring to Vicars' former friendship with Shackleton, but he was certain that he possessed a complete answer to such a complaint.

'I replied,' he wrote of this interview, 'that my brother had believed this man to be a man of good character, and that I presumed this man's other friends, including Lord Ronald Gower, the Duke of Argyll and the Bishop of Peterborough, believed the same.'

To this neither Lord Aberdeen nor Birrell made any comment; but at this second interview the latter admitted that this charge of associating with a man of undesirable character had, along with the accusation of negligence, been laid before the King. O'Mahony asked Lord Aberdeen to formulate in more detail the real accusations made against his brother; but the Lord-Lieutenant, mournful as a lost wolf-hound, enigmatic as the Sphinx, made no reply.

By this time Birrell was convinced that, if Vicars was dismissed and demanded a public inquiry, one would have to be set up; but he still hoped that he might be able to avoid taking such drastic steps. He believed that, if it could be shown that Shackleton was responsible for the theft, Vicars might be allowed to remain in office. With this object in mind, Dougherty was instructed to ask that all telegrams despatched by Shackleton between 6th July and 29th October might be produced. On 4th November, the Postmaster-General, replying to the request made by the Home Secretary, hoped that 'it is not the intention of the Secretary of State that search should be made among the forms of telegrams handed in at the whole of the Telegraph Offices in London during the period specified, and that it will be sufficient if search is made . . . at the South Audley Street and St James's Post Offices'.[1] These were the offices nearest to the addresses most frequently used by Shackleton – 44 Park Lane; the Royal Societies Club, St James's Street, and the Junior Army and Navy Club, St James's Street.

[1] Home Office File 156, 610/16.

Twelve telegrams were unearthed but none of them contained any reference 'to the criminal matter in respect of which their production was desired'. Dougherty was told that the original forms could not be allowed to leave the Home Office, but they would be shown to any person nominated by the Lord-Lieutenant. On the cover of the memorandum in the Home Office file some member of the staff wrote, on 6th November: 'If we allow these telegrams to go to Dublin Castle we do not know who may see them, or what may leak out.' In the end, Kane inspected the forms but 'could find nothing bearing in any way on the robbery'.[1] All the telegrams were held to refer to Shackleton's private affairs.

The authorities in Dublin now took a surprising step. They told Vicars that, if he would resign, he would be granted a pension. This failed to satisfy O'Mahony who promised to pay Vicars the equivalent of the proffered pension if he would refuse the offer. Thus it was that Vicars spurned with contempt this and subsequent approaches of the same kind. Lord Aberdeen now felt that he himself must persuade Vicars to see reason. While Birrell was in London, the Lord-Lieutenant received Vicars and his lawyer, Mr Meredith.

It is to George Wyndham, Birrell's predecessor as Irish Secretary, that we owe an account of this interview. It will be remembered that it was he who had brought Sir Anthony Macdonnell to Ireland; and there can be little doubt that it was from Macdonnell that he gleaned the story he told to Wilfrid Scawen Blunt in the following January. Recording the conversation he had with Wyndham, Scawen Blunt wrote: 'Lord Aberdeen has made himself a laughing stock at Dublin. . . . Vicars had gone to him and had bullied him, and had chivvied Aberdeen round the room when he had said that he could not give an answer [to Vicars' request for a public inquiry] without consulting Birrell.[2]'

A further interview, this time between Lord Aberdeen and Birrell on the one side, and Vicars and Mr Meredith on the other, is mentioned in a letter sent to the Lord-Lieutenant by O'Mahony early in December. Once again he pointed out that

---

[1] Home Office File 156, 610/16

[2] *My Diaries*, by Wilfrid Scawen Blunt (Martin Secker, London), Vol. II, pp. 192–3.

grave and unfounded charges had been brought against his brother, while matters which would exculpate Vicars had been deliberately suppressed.

'I am also aware' (continued O'Mahony) 'that, owing to the incontinence of official tongues, scandalous matters are being gossiped about in Dublin to my brother's detriment. . . . Your Excellency and Mr Birrell, at the interview with my brother and Mr Meredith, offered to put in writing that there was no question of my brother's integrity regarding the Jewels. If Your Excellency will add to that the above declaration regarding his moral character, I should be happy to lay the matter before my brother and his friends with a view to considering how far such a letter would vindicate my brother's character. I personally am determined to leave no stone unturned to bring the true state of affairs under the notice of His Majesty, and I now definitely ask Your Excellency to convey to His Majesty my humble request for an audience at which I may be allowed to state my brother's side of the case.'

Lord Aberdeen, averse from the start to any kind of public inquiry into matters touching his viceregal court, had always hoped that Macdonnell's plan would bear fruit; but now, as Birrell came increasingly under fire in the Commons from those Irish members who were not prepared always to toe Redmond's line, the Lord-Lieutenant realised that such an inquiry would have to take place. He therefore asked King Edward if he would authorise the setting up of a Court of Inquiry to examine all the circumstances relating to the theft of the Jewels. To this the King replied that he had no alternative but to agree to this proposal. Even after that, however, Lord Aberdeen continued to seek a formula by which Vicars might be persuaded to resign his office and retire without further ado. Since, so far as the King knew, no further steps were taken, Lord Knollys wrote to the Lord-Lieutenant on 4th December to say that: 'The King was complaining of the affair dragging on for five years . . .' and ended by saying that His Majesty now 'washed his hands of the whole affair'.[1]

The letter drove the agitated but still reluctant Viceroy to make one last bid to secure Vicars' resignation. On 7th Decem-

[1] *King Edward VII, A Biography*, by Sir Sidney Lee (Macmillan & Co., London, 1927), Vol. II, p. 474.

ber he wrote to O'Mahony to say that, unless Vicars resigned by the 9th, his office would be declared vacant by a notice in the *Dublin Gazette* on Tuesday, 10th December.

On the 9th, Macdonnell wrote to acknowledge O'Mahony's letter to Lord Aberdeen, and told him that his account of the meeting between the Lord-Lieutenant and Mr Birrell, Vicars and Mr Meredith, was inaccurate. He continued:

> The whole responsibility for the decision rests with the Irish Government and with the Irish Government alone, and therefore the introduction of the King's name into your letter is out of place and improper.

Ignoring Macdonnell, O'Mahony wrote directly to Lord Aberdeen, pointing out that, as it was Birrell who had first introduced the King's name into the discussion, he himself could not be blamed for doing so. Then, leaving the sting in the tail, he added:

> I am convinced that my brother is being sacrificed in order to shield others really culpable.

It is scarcely surprising that, although Vicars never tendered his resignation, no announcement as to his dismissal appeared in the *Gazette* of 10th December.

2

Although Peirce O'Mahony clearly enjoyed composing letters calculated to spread alarm and despondency in official circles, he realised that he must, if he was really to help his brother, enlist powerful supporters in his cause. He therefore drew up, with Vicars and Mr Meredith, a petition which he sent to all the Knights of St Patrick, asking them to append their signatures. Of the twenty-one Knights, sixteen signed the document and, of the remainder, Lord Howth was too ill to be approached, Lord Wolseley was abroad and the Earl of Kilmorey, Viscount Iveagh and Lord Clonbrock declined to add their names but wrote letters which O'Mahony forwarded with the petition to Lord Aberdeen. This suggests that the three reluctant peers expressed themselves in terms not entirely unfavourable to

Vicars. This petition, now preserved at the Home Office, was drawn up in the following terms:

To The King's Most Excellent Majesty
The Humble Petition of
The Knights of the Most Illustrious Order of St Patrick
Sheweth

That it has been brought to the notice of the Companions of Your Majesty's Most Illustrious Order of St Patrick that His Excellency the Grand Master has received Your Majesty's approval of the reconstitution of the Office of Arms, Dublin Castle, which will involve Ulster King of Arms being relieved of the Office which he now holds.

That having regard to the fact that Ulster King of Arms, as Executive Officer of the Order, in addition to his other heraldic duties, has invariably discharged his functions for the last fifteen years in a manner which has called forth the special approbation of the various Grand Masters of the Order under whom he served, and has received the signal commendation of Their Royal Highnesses The Prince of Wales, K.P., and the Duke of Connaught, K.P.

That Your Petitioners feel that an inquiry into all the circumstances connected with the recent disappearance of the Insignia of the Order, at which Ulster may be given an opportunity of being heard before any steps be taken to relieve him from his office, would be only fair and just.

Your Petitioners therefore humbly pray that Your Majesty may be graciously pleased to direct such an inquiry to be held.

The signatories were the Marquesses of Ormonde and Waterford, the Earls of Gosford, Carysfort, Erne, Bandon, Mayo, Listowel, Dunraven, Rosse, Lucan, Longford, Enniskillen and Meath, F.M. Earl Roberts and Lord Monteagle of Brandon.

In forwarding this document to Lord Aberdeen, O'Mahony asked that it might be transmitted to the King for his personal consideration; but on 14th December Sir James Dougherty returned it, saying that the Lord-Lieutenant could not see his way to forward it to His Majesty. Nevertheless it seems probable that the contents of the petition and the names of those who signed it were made known to the King, since Field-Marshal Lord Roberts very soon telegraphed from Windsor asking that his name might be removed from the petition. It would appear that the great soldier had been subjected to a short course of regal indoctrination.

But O'Mahony was not to be put off. The petition was altogether too powerful a weapon to lay aside unused, so he sent it to the Home Secretary with a request that a public inquiry might be held. At the same time, invoking the statutes of the Order of St Patrick, he humbly prayed that King Edward would grant his protection to Vicars at this time. Mr Gladstone, the Home Secretary, acknowledged this letter on 21st December and, two days later, O'Mahony sent him a further request that a public inquiry might be held. With this he enclosed a detailed statement of the various proceedings which had followed the disappearance of the Crown Jewels.

'I believe,' he wrote in his covering letter, 'on reading them you will agree with me that they constitute a case which no Government can afford to ignore. I would also beg of you to ascertain Lord Aberdeen's private opinion of the case as distinguished from that of the Irish Government as officially expressed.'

In the accompanying statement he made, among others, the following points:

> That Ulster now holds 'during good behaviour' and that it is without precedent to remove anyone so holding without a public and judicial inquiry.
>
> That the report which led to the proposal to reconstitute the Office of Arms was the product of a secret inquiry, held behind Ulster's back and that he was given no opportunity of defending himself at that inquiry, nor since.
>
> That he has never been informed of the nature or substance of the charges brought against him.
>
> That from the position of the safe . . . it is quite clear that the robbery could not have taken place during office hours. . . .

That it was no part of Ulster's original duty to have the custody of the Jewels. . . .

That under the new Statutes in 1905 they were consigned to the care of Ulster, who never received any pay for this onerous duty, and therefore ought to be regarded as a voluntary trustee.

That a trustee is never by law required to take better care of his trust property than an ordinary man takes of his own property.

That if the authorities required Ulster to take expert care of the Jewels, such as is required from a bank manager, they should have laid down regulations to that effect. . . .

Then, of the charge that Vicars had been an associate of Shackleton, O'Mahony pointed out that the latter 'must have been in his ordinary conduct a gentleman and not likely to attract suspicion'. He continued:

That for 15 years Ulster has devoted his life to the Office of Arms and spent his private capital in amassing a large private library of a technical character to assist him in his work, 1,500 volumes of which are at the Castle for the public and official use.

That from the nature of his work he is now unfitted to seek other employment and, if deprived of his position of Ulster, he will be driven out penniless and broken.

These arguments much impressed Mr Gladstone; and, in the following month, the *Pall Mall Gazette* reported that:

The whole question was discussed at the Cabinet, it being proposed by one Minister to insert a clause in the King's Speech – not, of course, intended to find a place there, but, as suggested at the meeting, to keep the necessary discussion to the one aspect of the advisability or not of further enquiry.

. . . A high official of the Home Office expressed strong views about the delay in transmitting the Knights' petition, and will urge the granting of a full inquiry, so as to save a vote of censure in Parliament and a Cabinet crisis.

This high official can only have been Herbert Gladstone; and it was largely due to his initiative that, after a Christmas holding little of peace or good will for those chiefly concerned with the lost Crown Jewels, a Commission of Inquiry was set up. King Edward's biographer records the fact in the following terms:[1]

> On January 6th a commission was appointed to investigate the matter. . . . The whole episode showed extreme incapacity on the part of the Irish Government. Neither the Irish Secretary, Mr Birrell, nor the Under Secretary, Sir Anthony Mac-Donnell, nor, above all, the Lord-Lieutenant came well out of the matter. The King's anger was fully justified.

[1] *King Edward VII, A Biography*, by Sir Sidney Lee (Macmillan & Co., London, 1972), Vol. II, p. 474.

CHAPTER TWO

Some time before this, however, Peirce O'Mahony had decided to find out whether the ultra-Nationalists would help him in the fight. Arthur Griffith was at this time publishing a newspaper, *Sinn Fein*, in an office in D'Olier Street. A strange man in whom a strong streak of romanticism was blended with the capacity to exploit quite ruthlessly every opportunity tending to further the cause of Irish freedom, he was to become the chief architect of the Irish republic.

On his staff was one J.W. O'Beirne who, as a result of Fenian activities, had once been sentenced to a long term of imprisonment in an English gaol, from which Parnell and O'Mahony had succeeded in obtaining his release. O'Beirne was a man endowed with the grace of gratitude. Now, in the hour of O'Mahony's need, he was anxious to help him. In preliminary discussions between O'Mahony and O'Beirne it was decided that a small group should concert plans to embarrass the Government and bring about the appointment of a Commission of Inquiry.

So, on a winter's day, O'Beirne, Arthur Griffith and another man[1] travelled down to the green lands of County Wicklow. O'Mahony met them at the station and drove them out to Grange Con, where a sumptuous Edwardian luncheon had been prepared. Either during that meal or during the subsequent discussion O'Mahony told his guests a story which makes clear many of the problems connected with the larceny of the Crown Jewels.

If Vicars' position had not been so critical it is doubtful whether O'Mahony would have told his guests all that he did. He knew they would have heard the rumours current in Dublin about the drink parties Vicars occasionally gave at the Office of Arms. He had, also, seen how the charges raised by Macdonnell against Vicars had made Redmond refuse his support for a public inquiry. But desperate needs demand desperate measures; and O'Mahony believed that the whole truth, so far as he knew it, must now be revealed.

[1] Believed to have been Mr Bulmer Hobson.

It was of these parties that he now spoke. They were in no way remarkable for their depravity but were, rather, a striking example of hope triumphing over experience. For the truth was that Vicars was incapable of carrying more than a very little drink. Even a couple of glasses of sherry were sufficient not only to cloud his intellect but to bring him to the verge of unconsciousness. So he rarely drank more than a token glass at any time. There were occasions, however, when he permitted himself to depart from this abstemious rule.

At one of these parties in the Bedford Tower, O'Mahony told his guests, Vicars had suddenly collapsed to the floor, lying there inert and unconscious. In an age as partial as was that to elaborate practical jokes it was almost certain that someone would use so golden an opportunity to make the pompous Vicars appear an ass. A member of the viceregal staff – whom O'Mahony named – bent down and removed Ulster's keys from his person. Then, explaining to the others what he intended to do, he opened the safe and removed the badge and star of the Order, afterwards returning the keys to their host's pockets. Remembering the confidence with which Vicars expected the insignia and collars to be returned to him through the post, there seems little doubt that it was thus that the practical joker returned the diamonds on this earlier occasion. It also seems certain that Lord Aberdeen knew of that regrettable joke.

He was, of course, not the only one to have heard that story. The charm of the Irish, as a race, is tempered with a malicious insight into the characters and foibles of those, even, whom they sincerely like and admire. So it is not surprising that news of these happenings should have reached the ears of two men who saw in it a means of obtaining the money which, according to O'Mahony, both needed so desperately. At Grange Con that day the two men were stated to be Francis Shackleton and Captain Richard Howard Gorges.

It is to be regretted that we have no trustworthy account of all that passed that day at Grange Con. Two stories were to be published later which appear to have been based on O'Mahony's revelations to his guests. One of these, published after Vicars' death, was evidently written by someone whose memory was at fault. It is so full of inaccuracies that one would hesitate to accept any part as true, were it not that it bears a strong resemblance to the other version, as well as to the rumoured content of Peirce O'Mahony's statement to his guests. Having mentioned briefly the loss of the Jewels, the writer referred to Vicars' friendship with Shackleton, whom he describes as 'a man who had all the outward marks of a gentleman'. He continued:

> On the evening of July 5th Sir Arthur gave a supper party to several of his friends, including the man referred to. This man, with consummate art and tact, had managed to win his way back into the regard of Sir Arthur – a proof of his amazingly attractive nature. He brought a stranger to the party, of whom the less said the better.
>
> At about 2 in the morning the party broke up, and Sir Arthur, who complained of feeling unusually drowsy, was assisted to his bedroom. He was helped to bed by the supposed friend. Round his neck he wore a fine steel chain. Secured to it were the two tiny keys that opened the strong room and the iron chest. Is it difficult to see what happened?
>
> ... The very next day an accommodating Dublin locksmith who had a shop in a small street opening out of Sackville Street, made two keys from wax impressions supplied, and unquestionably the very next evening the room was opened and the box rifled of a part of the contents.[1]

Much of this is manifest nonsense. The dates mentioned must be wrong; and Kane's investigations left no doubt in his own mind that Shackleton could not have been in Dublin during the period he claimed to have spent in England. There is, however, a sufficient resemblance between this story and that we will examine presently to suggest that both had a common origin in whatever was told by Peirce O'Mahony over his luncheon table at Grange Con. Vicars may very well have been drugged or made drunk shortly before the loss of the Jewels was discovered, even though the date must have been earlier than 5th July. As we shall see, Vicars himself, writing of the man 'of whom the less said the better', and against whom he had warned Shackleton, says enough to suggest that this regrettable incident could have taken place on 30th June. It is at any rate certain that Peirce O'Mahony's disclosures must have been based on information he had obtained – not, one may suppose,

---

[1] From a press cutting in an album kept by Mr Fuller.

without a good deal of persistence and trouble – from Vicars himself.

The second account appeared in the *Gaelic American* on 4th July, 1908. This is believed to have been written by Mr Bulmer Hobson. Not only was he writing articles for the paper at that time, and is said to have been one of the guests at Grange Con, but the whole article bears the imprint of that rather muddled kindliness which still prevents him from telling what he knows of the affair. Thus, although he was not unwilling to rake up much unsavoury history from the past of a man who must, to many living at that time, have been easily identifiable as Captain Gorges, Mr Hobson evidently hoped that no one would recognise that sinister figure if he transmuted the name to the very improbable 'Gaudeans'. Similarly, although the author was not averse to titillating the imaginations of his readers with talk of orgies and abominations, he seems to have accepted without question the picture drawn by O'Mahony of Vicars as a very gentle, perfect knight who was totally unaware of the activities practised by his associates after he had left the Office.

Under a banner headline, 'ABOMINATIONS OF DUBLIN CASTLE EXPOSED', the circumstances of the theft and the course of the subsequent inquiry are reviewed briefly. Then, after mentioning Shackleton's appointment as Dublin Herald, the writer continued:

> He appeared to be a gentleman of good repute and was on visiting terms with Lord Aberdeen and many of the aristocracy. Mr Shackleton, however, was a man well known to the police. Around his name had gathered a lot of very unsavory rumors. Some of his associates, titled and untitled, were men suspected of unspeakable and disgusting offences.
>
> Sir Arthur Vicars ... did not know anything of this, but the authorities with whom rested the appointment can hardly have been ignorant of it. The English police had a record of his career at Scotland Yard. Yet he was appointed by the English Government to a post in Ireland.
>
> After his arrival rumors began to circulate in Dublin that there were nightly orgies at the Castle, in which several prominent Government officials were mixed up. ...
>
> The whispered stories were true. There took place in the Castle abominable orgies in which these persons took part.

THE UNSPEAKABLE CAPTAIN GAUDEANS

Among those who were not Castle officials there was one
Captain Gaudeans, a man known to the English police, a man
of absolutely depraved character, yet a constant associate of
English Government officials in Ireland. This man's history is
too long and too filthy to be gone into here. One incident from
his past will suffice. During the late English–Boer War,
Gaudeans was a trooper in Thorneycroft's Horse on active
service against the Boers. When on campaign he was caught
red-handed committing a bestial crime.

He was arrested and the officer who made the arrest reported to General Thorneycroft and asked him if he would
court-martial Gaudeans. 'Shoot the brute; I wouldn't try
him,' replied Thorneycroft. The officer pointed out that they
could hardly have the man shot without a trial. 'Then kick him
out of the regiment,' answered the General. The regiment was
drawn up in two lines, facing inwards, and Gaudeans was
marched out. As he passed every man in the regiment had a
kick at him, and he was seen no more by Thorneycroft's Horse.

Gaudeans returned to England, now holds a commission in
the English army and is at the present time a musketry instructor at Portsmouth, England. Last year he was sent over to
Ireland in the summer months to superintend the musketry
drill of some militia regiments.

O'Mahony's guests must have listened to his tale with a
deepening sense of disappointment. Here was just such a story
as they had always longed to have in order to bludgeon and to
prick their English masters wherever it would hurt them most.
But could any of these statements be proved? Would anyone
who had taken part in these alleged orgies be willing to describe
what had taken place? To twist the tail of the British lion was
one thing. To endanger by a libel action the very existence of
their paper was quite another. And for whose benefit were they
to run such risks? For Arthur Vicars, the devoted servant of
the English Crown, the man whose professional duties required
him to forge new chains of tawdry gilt to bind the upper classes
in Ireland ever more closely to the King. Besides, could anyone
believe, as O'Mahony evidently hoped they would, that Vicars
had been so much immersed in his genealogical and heraldic
studies that he had never noticed what was now said to be
Shackleton's ruling interest?

They probably did not tell O'Mahony of their increasing doubts but, just as Redmond had been persuaded by Birrell's vague charges against Vicars' moral character to withdraw his support for O'Mahony's campaign, so now Arthur Griffith and his colleagues, men who constantly declaimed against Redmond's pusillanimity and subservience to the English Government, decided that, at least for the time being, they too must do nothing to help Vicars.

BOOK FOUR

❧

The Inquiry

CHAPTER ONE

1

The New Year brought resolution to Lord Aberdeen's reluctant hand. On 6th January, Dougherty appended his signature to the following document.

> By the Lord-Lieutenant-General and General Governor of Ireland
> ABERDEEN –
>
> Whereas we have deemed it expedient that a Committee should issue forthwith to investigate the circumstances of the loss of the Regalia of the Order of St Patrick and to inquire whether Sir Arthur Vicars exercised due vigilance and proper care as the custodian thereof.
>
> Now We, John Campbell, Earl of Aberdeen, Lord-Lieutenant-General and General Governor of Ireland, nominate, constitute and appoint you, His Honour James Johnston Shaw, Robert Fitzwilliam Starkie, Esquire, and Chester Jones, Esquire, to be Commissioners for the purpose of the said Inquiry.
>
> We do by these presents authorise and empower you to inquire of and concerning the premises, and to examine witnesses, and call for and examine all such books and documents as you shall judge likely to afford you the fullest information and to report to Us what you shall find touching and concerning the premises.
>
> Given at His Majesty's Castle in Dublin this 6th day of January, 1908.

When this was issued to the Press, it was regarded by most as a considerable triumph for Vicars and O'Mahony, because many understood, as did *The Times* of 9th January, that: 'The Commission . . . is empowered to take evidence on oath'. This is exactly what the Commission was not authorised to do: and it was upon this point that so fierce a storm of controversy was going to be aroused during the subsequent proceedings.

On the same day O'Mahony issued a denial of the report, published in an English newspaper, that Vicars had resigned his post as Ulster King of Arms. O'Mahony made it quite clear that his stepbrother had no intention of resigning.

The Commission of Inquiry met for the first time on 10th January. Seldom can an investigation of this kind have taken place upon the actual scene of the crime; but here the empty safe still stood as a mute reminder of why the distinguished and official persons were gathering that morning within the library of the Office of Arms. Here was the Solicitor-General for Ireland, Mr Redmond Barry, K.C., M.P., conferring with the Chief Crown Solicitor, Mr Malachi Kelly. There were Vicars' counsel, the brilliant and striking-looking J. H. Campbell,[1] K.C., M.P., and Mr Timothy M. Healy,[2] K.C., M.P., who, after years of estrangement from O'Mahony, had now consented to act with Mr Campbell on Vicars' behalf. Both Press and public were rigorously excluded from the hearing.

At the outset Mr Campbell asked if the Inquiry was to be held in private or whether the public were to be admitted. The Chairman replied that the Commission would sit in private, although the Commissioners would listen to any application Mr Campbell might care to make. The latter then formally requested that the Inquiry should be held in public, and went on to criticise the wording of the Lord-Lieutenant's Warrant, pointing out that it neither empowered the Commissioners to compel the attendance of witnesses nor to examine them upon oath.

'It would be an intolerable act of injustice,' he declared, 'to have an inquiry which would appear to exclude consideration of the very terrible suggestions and insinuations affecting the moral character of Sir Arthur Vicars, though it is notorious that they were part and parcel of the information upon which action was taken in the month of October last.' Mr Campbell then explained that one of the charges brought against his client, 'not formulated but insinuated against him, is an allegation that

[1] (1851–1931) Lord Chief Justice of Ireland, 1916–18; Lord Chancellor of Ireland, 1918–21. Created Lord Glenavy; Chairman of the Irish Free State Senate.
[2] (1853–1951) First Governor-General of the Irish Free State, 1922–7.

he introduced an undesirable person into the privacy of his office'. Then, speaking of the actual disappearance of the Jewels, he said:

'This is a crime which is alleged to have baffled the police from the date of its commission up to the present.'

To which Mr Chester Jones replied, 'We are not here to find out who the thief was. That is a job for the police.'

The Chairman, Judge Shaw, hastened to confirm this interpretation of their instructions.

'We are not investigating the crime . . . ' he explained, 'I do not think the reference gives us any such power whatever.'

Those present had scarcely time to wonder what display of action or inaction the Commissioners would give if their inquiries should elicit undoubted proof of the thief's identity, when their thoughts were jolted back from the speculative to the actual. For Mr Campbell now took a formidable step. Declaring that it was all too clear that Vicars was to be allowed no opportunity to vindicate his character or to repel the unformulated accusations which were the real cause of his dismissal, Mr Campbell announced that neither Vicars nor his Counsel could recognise the validity or the usefulness of the inquiry. They would therefore take no further part in the proceedings. It was a moment of high drama such as even the Irish Courts have seldom seen.

At last the Solicitor-General spoke, observing that a public judicial inquiry, of the kind envisaged by Mr Campbell, could not be set up without the sanction of Parliament.

'Why not ask Parliament for it?' asked Mr Campbell. 'We will support you in Parliament.'

Ignoring this most reasonable suggestion, the Solicitor-General suggested that Vicars would be failing in his duty as the appointed custodian of the regalia if he withdrew from the inquiry at this juncture.

Mr Campbell turned to Vicars and Peirce O'Mahony. Then, accompanied by Healy, they rose and bowed to the Commissioners. As they moved towards the door, held open for them by an usher, the room was completely silent. Without a backward glance Vicars went out into the hall. It was a fine dramatic gesture, but not yet would the final curtain be rung down.

The Commissioners now debated what they should do. Their report mentions the difficulties in which they found themselves.

> On the withdrawal of Sir Arthur Vicars ... we were disposed to think that no useful purpose could be served by the prosecution of the Inquiry.... But when the Solicitor-General, on behalf of the Government, asked us to hear his evidence relevant to our Inquiry which he was in a position to offer, and assured us he was in possession of important evidence in both branches of our Inquiry, we felt that we could not refuse to receive and record the evidence thus tendered, and that we must leave the responsibility for any deficiencies in the evidence on those who refused to take part in our proceedings.

Meanwhile, as the Commissioners decided to continue their work, the representatives of the Press, debarred from attending the Inquiry, received Vicars and his friends with enthusiasm. To them Vicars handed a statement he had brought with him. In consequence, on the following day, the papers united in presenting his case in a most favourable light, while the Government was attacked for the air of mystery with which they had invested the whole affair. This, it was suggested, could only be explained if the identity of the thief was already known to the Government but was not to be disclosed to the public.

Meanwhile the Commissioners, their initial doubts resolved, were quite satisfied. As they were to remark rather smugly in their Report:

> We had the advantage ... of the written statements made by Sir Arthur Vicars to the police and of the oral statements made by him at various times to the police and other witnesses examined before us.

For five days the Commission received evidence. They heard the stories told by all but two of the staff of the Office of Arms. Mr Horlock and Miss Gibbon refused to attend, saying that they felt Vicars 'was not getting fair play'. This unexpected repulse drew no comment from the Commissioners, who went on to hear the evidence of the many police officers who had taken any part in the investigation. Among these was Chief Inspector Kane of Scotland Yard.

The charge that Vicars had been negligent in his guardianship of the Crown Jewels was firmly based upon a reading of the revised Statutes of the Order of St Patrick. Thus it was clearly shown that, although laid down that the jewelled Insignia and the badges and collars of the Knights were to be deposited for safe-keeping 'in a steel safe in the strong-room in the Chancery of the Order', the safe was kept permanently in the library, the room most used by casual visitors to the Bedford Tower. Besides, as the Solicitor-General pointed out, at the time of the theft three gold collars and badges belonging to the Knights, two state maces, the Irish Sword of State, a jewelled sceptre, a crown and two massive silver spurs, were exposed to view in a glass case in the strong-room, while another gold collar lay in a drawer in the same place. Vicars' statements to the police on these matters were read. Then Sir George Holmes was questioned about the correspondence between Ulster and himself after it was found that the safe would not go through the door of the newly-built strong-room.

The Solicitor-General now turned to the vexed and complicated question of the various keys and their holders. It was now that Detective Officer Kerr became so confused that he invented a fifth key to the strong-room, a mistake which brought no comment from anyone except that Judge Shaw exclaimed in tones of deep satisfaction, 'That clears up the only difficulty I had'. Some muddled realisation that they had not, perhaps, quite understood all they had been told about the keys may have led the Commissioners in their report to upbraid Vicars rather pettishly for the arrangements he had made as to their safe keeping.

> They stated that they could not 'arrive at the conclusion that Sir Arthur Vicars exercised due vigilance in the custody of the Jewels. . . . We should have thought that in the case of Jewels like these of immense value and of national importance, the responsible custodian would, instead of carrying about the key of the safe in his pocket, have deposited it with his banker or in some other place of security except on the rare occasions when it was in use. We are of opinion that great want of proper care was also shown in respect of the Strong Room. . . . We have been unable to ascertain any sufficient reason why a key of the Strong Room should have been in any hands but Sir Arthur Vicars' own. . . .

They failed to realise that, had Vicars deposited the keys with his banker, he would have violated the statutes of the Order by surrendering the custody of the Jewels to an unauthorised person. The suggestion that only Vicars should have held a key to the strong-room would have been quite impractical since he would have had to open and close the door each time a member of the staff wished to refer to any of the books or manuscripts kept therein.

The Commissioners from there went on to state that they could not 'attribute negligence to Sir Arthur Vicars in the custody of his key of the strong-room. He seems to have taken as much care of it as any man could do of a key which he carried about with him, and which was in constant use.' Nevertheless they thought 'it was an imprudent thing to give a key of the strong-room to a man in Stivey's position, though we are fully convinced of Stivey's probity'.

This faint praise can have been of little comfort to one already condemned to the Wesleyan Soldiers' Home, though it makes one wonder anew upon what grounds Stivey had been dismissed so summarily. The former messenger had returned briefly to his old haunts as the Solicitor-General required his testimony on several points.

The evidence given by Mrs Farrell produced one item of interest, though it was not until April, 1908, when Birrell made an unexpected statement in the House of Commons, that the office cleaner's words acquired especial significance. Now, after Mrs Farrell had left the witness-stand and Horlock had declined to give evidence, the Commissioners prepared themselves to receive the evidence of Francis Bennett-Goldney.

2

On his arrival in Dublin, Goldney had not, this time, gone at once to St James's Terrace. Instead he had booked a room at the Shelbourne Hotel. This was in character, for Goldney was an ambitious man who intended to remain on good terms with the authorities. It would never have entered his mind to show himself a friend of one already living within the shadow of official disapproval.

When Lord Aberdeen had requested the staff of the Office of Arms to resign, Goldney had not even waited to consult Vicars before agreeing to do so. He gave his own account of the transaction in a letter to *The Times* on 8th November, 1909.

> I resigned the Office of my own free will. Lord Aberdeen has my letters which I wrote to him at the time, telling him my only wish was to facilitate by any means in my power, whatever steps he might desire to take for the recovery of what I considered a national loss. For, apart from the intrinsic value of the gold and jewels, the beautiful enamelling of the old collars can never be replaced.

Exactly how his so ready acceptance of Lord Aberdeen's request was to help materially in the recovery of the regalia is still obscure.

After he had settled in at the Shelbourne, Goldney called on Vicars' lawyers. To his intense embarrassment he found that Vicars was in conference with Mr Meredith, the head of the firm. He therefore sent a message by a clerk asking if he might speak to the lawyer privately. Meredith agreed and, after a short conversation with Goldney, returned to Vicars. Almost at once he went to Goldney, bringing a message to the effect that Sir Arthur would like to offer his English friend some hospitality. Although Vicars must have had a great deal upon his mind, he continued to exhibit the most impeccable manners.

'I said,' Goldney found an opportunity of telling the Commissioners, 'that I would rather not, as I did not intend to call on Sir Arthur during my visit to Dublin, as I felt it would be better if I did not. I do not want you to think that I have been seeing Sir Arthur privately.'

In the course of his examination by the Solicitor-General, Goldney confessed to finding himself in something of a difficulty, though it was clearly one from which he derived no small pleasure. After giving a rambling account of the visits he had paid to Dublin since his appointment as Athlone Pursuivant, he told how he had been present on two occasions when Vicars had shown the Crown Jewels to visitors to the Office. Then he said how, when he had come over for the Dublin Horse Show, he had found Vicars much run down and in need of a change. He had therefore asked him to stay at Abbots Barton.

'I do not know,' he confided to the Commissioners, 'how much to say or how little, or how I would be justified in stating things that might only tend to raise suspicions. I do not suspect anybody as being guilty of taking the Jewels – though I suspect certain persons may know something about it.'

Having thus loosed the pebble of insinuation into the pool of public conjecture, Goldney made a statement which the Commissioners decided was not relevant to the inquiry, and the Chairman ordered that it should be struck from the record. After which, as if to demonstrate that there was no ill-feeling between himself and Vicars, Goldney remarked that he had thought Ulster was 'always fussily careful of the Office'.

3

Goldney was succeeded on the witness-stand by Mr Harrel, Assistant Commissioner of the Dublin Metropolitan Police. He was questioned about his visit to the Office of Arms on 6th July, and about his subsequent conversations with Vicars.

'Did he,' asked the Chairman, 'in any of these conversations express suspicion with regard to any particular person? I do not want you to name the person – but did he mention that he suspected anyone?'

'Yes,' replied Harrel, 'he mentioned one person; but I must say that, after full enquiry, we found there was no foundation for his suspicions. I am absolutely satisfied of that, and I may say that Sir Arthur Vicars himself altogether abandoned suspicion afterwards.'

When the Solicitor-General proceeded to ask if Vicars' coachman, Phillips, had ever had access to his master's keys, it at once became apparent that it was he whose name the Chairman had hoped to keep secret. The Assistant Commissioner explained that Phillips could not be produced as a witness as Vicars had paid his fare to America. The Commissioners appear to have shown neither surprise nor interest at this remarkable piece of information. They next turned their attention to the various people to whom Ulster was said to have shown the Crown Jewels, and to the record of visitors which Stivey had kept.

Harrel now disclosed that it had not been until 12th November that Vicars had admitted that he had shown the regalia to more persons than he had told the police at first. He mentioned

Mr Esmé Percy, Mrs Brown-Potter and Miss Newman, a friend of Horlock.

'May I ask,' inquired the Solicitor-General, 'do you know anything of Miss Newman?'

'Yes,' was the surprising answer. 'I know everything about her. What I want to make clear is, I would like to draw some line between what exactly relates to the circumstance under which the jewels were lost, and the police inquiry which was made subsequently from a criminal point of view.'

Then, having successfully indicated that Vicars had not been sufficiently careful about those to whom he showed the Crown Jewels, the Solicitor-General led Harrel to discuss the custody of the various keys. But these late-named visitors to the Office of Arms had already figured in Stivey's evidence. Questioning the former messenger about his rather incompetent way of keeping the Visitors' Book, the Solicitor-General asked if Stivey could remember Mrs Brown-Potter visiting the Office of Arms with Mr Esmé Percy. Stivey said he remembered the occasion, but he had not entered the lady's name in the book. He was in the habit of entering only one name, even though there were several visitors arriving together. He knew that Mrs Brown-Potter and Mr Percy had come to the Office with Vicars, but he did not know whether or not they had been shown the Crown Jewels. Another time Mr Percy had visited the Castle with a different lady. In answer to a further question, Stivey said he had every reason to believe that Mr Percy was at that time staying with Vicars in St James's Terrace.

When asked if he knew a Miss Daisy Newman, the former messenger told the Solicitor-General that he did not. Finally, encouraged by his inquisitor, he remembered a visit from a lady whose name he had never heard. It had been in April, 1907, and she had come more than once with Mr Horlock. On one occasion Vicars had taken her and Horlock into the strongroom, but he could not say whether Sir Arthur had shown her the Crown Jewels.

Stivey was then asked to tell the Commission how he had learnt Mrs Brown-Potter's name. He said that Vicars had told him that 'the police had been inquiring about Mr Esmé Percy as they had got him in the book, and he said "Have you got him in the book?" and I said, "I think I have, Sir Arthur." Sir

Arthur and I turned over the leaves of the journal of names and he turned up Mr Percy's name. Sir Arthur then said, "You have not Mrs Brown-Potter's here." I think that was the first time I have known the lady's name. I knew there was a lady with Mr Percy and I said, "Shall I put it in now?" and he said, "Don't make any alterations in the book now." '

On which prudent note Mrs Brown-Potter and Miss Daisy Newman fade into the obscurity from which, so briefly and to so little apparent purpose, their names had been drawn out by the Solicitor-General. It is only fair to remark that there was no evidence to suggest that either Mrs Brown-Potter or Mr Percy ever came into contact with the dubious Miss Newman.

Reverting now to Mr Harrel's evidence, the Solicitor-General, having discovered nothing new connected with the keys, asked the Assistant Commissioner about the routine guarding of the Castle by the military and the police. Harrel explained at some length how constant was the vigilance of the guards on all occasions; but he had to confess that neither the soldiers nor the police who had been on guard during the evening and throughout the night of 5th July had seen anything to arouse their suspicions, nor could any of them remember having seen Vicars leave the Castle.

CHAPTER TWO

1

When the Commission resumed its sitting on the following day, Goldney asked if he might be allowed to supplement the evidence he had already given. He took it for granted that the Commissioners must already know that, as he put it, there had been 'a little friction . . . between members in the Office owing to money, and it has always been over this question. I helped these people, honestly believing it was Sir Arthur Vicars' wish that I should do so.'

If one feels a certain exasperated pity for Goldney when he discovered, very soon after he became Athlone Pursuivant, that, in part at least, he owed this colourful title to the fact that he was a bachelor of ample means, this feeling diminishes as we read how, almost immediately after this passage in his evidence, he turned to the Solicitor-General and said:

'Please understand this, I do not want to prejudice you against any member of the Office.'

Because that is what Goldney most wished to do.

Certainly the story he had to tell the Commissioners was as curious as it was sordid. Some time before the disappearance of the Crown Jewels, and probably while Goldney had been in Dublin for the opening of the Irish Exhibition, Vicars had confided to him that he had entered into financial commitments he could not afford.

'If you are in money difficulties,' the amiable Goldney had told him, 'I hope you will come to me, because I will certainly try and help you.'

Perhaps a rather grandiose magnanimity becomes almost second nature to a Tory mayor; but it is doubtful whether Goldney had ever expected to be taken at his word. But Vicars explained that he had guaranteed two bills for Shackleton – one for £600, the other for £750 – and he hoped Goldney would accept responsibility for these.

It would have been extremely difficult for Goldney to refuse Vicars' request, in view of his own offer of help, but he did contrive to escape with signing only one bill, that for £600.

The exact sequence of the subsequent financial transactions is not easy to follow; but it must have been in June, shortly after Shackleton's arrival in England, that these entered upon their second dramatic phase.

Goldney had been spending a few days in Paris and, upon his return to Abbots Barton, his mother handed him a telegram. This announced that Shackleton would travel down to Canterbury that evening on the eight o'clock train. Nothing could have been calculated to spoil so much the homecoming of this rather smug prodigal. Goldney had never cared much for Shackleton, and he must have guessed the purport of this visit. He told the Commissioners of the explanation given to him when, upon that summer evening, Shackleton arrived at Abbots Barton.

'I am in a great hole,' the young man had told his reluctant host. 'I cannot go over to Ireland to see Sir Arthur Vicars, who has requested me to help him in this matter. It is merely a question of shares, and it must be done at once. I must have the money by Monday morning, and unless I can get somebody to do it I shall be in the greatest difficulty.'

He then asked Goldney to sign a bill for £1,500. This was to supersede the two bills for £600 and £750 which Vicars had backed originally. Goldney was not in the least anxious to give Shackleton any further financial assistance; and the latter had evidently expected this, as he had taken steps to meet such a contingency. He told Goldney that his family solicitor would be arriving later in the evening.

True enough, about half an hour later, a gentleman rang the bell at Abbots Barton. Only later was Goldney to discover that the newcomer was neither a solicitor nor a gentleman but the presiding genius of Messrs Wilton & Co., the moneylenders who held the bills guaranteed by Goldney and Vicars.

There is a suggestion of high Victorian melodrama as the masquerading usurer, carrying a large black bag, was shown into the library. As soon as Shackleton had made the introductions, the new arrival asked Goldney if he knew the nature of the business which had brought him there. To which the Mayor replied: 'I presume you have come about this business.'

Conversation did not flourish. It would seem that Goldney, with considerable perspicacity, viewed Shackleton's friend with almost as much dislike as distrust.

'You are Mayor of Canterbury?'

To which Goldney, usually so proud of his civic honours, replied with rare brusqueness.

'You must find that out from other people.'

Feeling, perhaps, that small talk would get him nowhere, the 'family solicitor' proceeded to business.

'Are you prepared to sign this bill?'

'I do not like it,' he told Shackleton, 'but, as it is to please Sir Arthur Vicars, and I am to be in his Office, I will do it.'

Thereupon his two visitors assured him that 'the whole thing was to be put square, and that it was only for a week at the most'.

The Commissioners had listened to Goldney's story in enthralled silence; but at this point the Chairman ventured to interrupt.

'To please Sir Arthur Vicars you signed this bill for Shackleton?'

'Yes,' replied Goldney. 'But it never was put straight, and there was a good deal of unpleasantness and difficulty about it.'

'It was merely by chance,' he went on, 'that I talked to Sir Arthur Vicars about money matters, and then he told me, "I never asked you to do it, and never wished you even to do it, and did not even know all the details." Then we began to compare notes, and I found out things that I had no idea of.'

It was as Goldney told the Commissioners that he had instructed Sir George Lewis to see that the bills were cancelled that the Chairman once more interrupted him.

'Somebody must have paid this bill if Shackleton did not?'

'Oh,' explained Goldney, 'Sir George Lewis insisted that it should be paid at once, because he was able to bring a certain amount of pressure, I suppose, and it was paid off. It was paid off, as a matter of fact, I believe, by Mr Shackleton's brother, but I do not know for certain, but they were both paid off together.'

The cancelled bills had been sent to Sir George Lewis in October, 1907.

Goldney now found an opportunity of mentioning the remark made by Shackleton at Lady Ormonde's luncheon party.

'The reason of his saying it was peculiar,' he said as he came to the end, 'but, I think, a perfectly straightforward one.'

At the end of that day's hearing, the Commissioners instructed their secretary to write to Vicars' lawyers. Mr Beard's letter, which was delivered to Mr Meredith on the following morning at eleven o'clock, stated that 'much evidence which, in the absence of any explanation or answer on the part of Sir Arthur Vicars, seriously affects him in his office as custodian of the Crown Jewels . . . ' had been given in the course of the hearing. The Commissioners hoped that Vicars would now attend the Inquiry. They wished him to have every opportunity of explaining those aspects of the evidence which still perplexed them.

At two o'clock in the afternoon a further letter was sent to the solicitors. In this Mr Beard declared that 'if Sir Arthur Vicars is ready to assist the Commission by his evidence, they have no objection, if he thinks it is desirable, to take his evidence in public, together with the evidence of any other witnesses whom he may think it desirable to have examined'.

This extraordinary *volte-face*, by which the Commissioners conceded the point they had hitherto so stubbornly refused to grant, was treated by Vicars with contempt. In his reply he repeated his objections to the Inquiry. At the same time he sent to the Press copies of Mr Beard's letters and his own reply. Next day the papers were almost unanimous in attacking both the Government and the Commissioners for the way in which the case was being handled. Only the *Morning Leader*, a London paper, suggested that Vicars' continued refusal to attend the Inquiry was more courageous than prudent.

2

While the Commissioners awaited the outcome of this new approach to Vicars, Harrel was recalled to the witness-stand. The Chairman explained that he and his colleagues were anxious to hear from the police all they knew regarding the movements of anyone who had access to the Office of Arms on the day preceding the discovery of the theft.

'While we are extremely unwilling,' Judge Shaw was careful to explain, 'to embark on anything that could be construed into a criminal investigation, or an idea that we were a Commission appointed to find out who was the author of this crime, we are of opinion that we are bound to investigate all the circumstances connected with the disappearance of the Jewels.'

Harrel, however, could give no further help except to assure them that Vicars had been at his home before eight o'clock on the evening of 5th July. He was succeeded at the stand by Mr Hodgson.

After relating how he had met Vicars and been invited to visit the Office of Arms, he said that he had been more interested in the blue garter, said to have belonged to the first Duke of Marlborough, than in the Crown Jewels. Someone else had been in the strong-room when these were taken from the safe. He thought it might have been Mr Burtchaell, but Vicars had not introduced him. He completed his evidence by giving some account of the letters and telegrams he had received from Vicars since the discovery of the theft.

He was followed by a number of police officers who, oddly enough, were asked nothing about the movements of the Office staff on 5th July. This aspect of the Inquiry appears to have been forgotten both by the Solicitor-General and the Commissioners. The interest of the latter was now concentrated upon the fragment of silk ribbon which had been left in the morocco case. Both Sir John Ross and Chief Inspector Kane were questioned about this.

Kane said this piece of silk confirmed him in his belief that the thief must either be a member of the staff or someone introduced by one of them. When he had told Vicars this, the latter had said repeatedly that he had 'implicit confidence in every member of my staff'. It was not until 30th August that Vicars, calling on Kane at Scotland Yard, had accused Shackleton of responsibility for the theft. After that, accompanied either by Goldney or by his brother, Major Vicars, Sir Arthur had frequently visited the Yard, each time repeating his accusations.

The Chief Inspector was asked nothing, and volunteered nothing, regarding the investigation he and his men had carried out in Dublin, nor who it was he had named as the criminal.

10

Instead he declared that he had never found the remotest shred of evidence against Shackleton.

'I have repeated to Sir Arthur Vicars,' he told the Commissioners, 'and his friends, over and over again, and I desire to say that now, when they pestered me with not only suggestions but direct accusations of Mr Shackleton, that they might as well accuse me, so far as the evidence they produced went to justify them.'

CHAPTER THREE

1

It was characteristic of Shackleton that, when the summons bidding him attend the Commission of Inquiry caught up with him, he should have been at San Remo with his friends, Lord Ronald Gower and Frank Hird. His financial affairs might be in a desperate condition, but he must be seen in the right places and with the right people. . . . The official letter from Dublin did not reach him until 11th January, the second day of the Inquiry; but, though he must have guessed that both Vicars and Goldney would say all they could to his discredit, he at once made arrangements to leave for Ireland. So, on the penultimate day of the Inquiry, those gathered in the library of the Office of Arms heard the usher call Mr Francis Richard Shackleton.

The first part of his interrogation dealt only with details of his career; but, when the Solicitor-General asked Shackleton about the financial arrangements made by Vicars and himself as co-tenants of the house in St James's Terrace, the answers were such as to quicken even the most flagging attention. An impression had been created by Goldney, as well as by remarks made by Vicars at various times, that Shackleton was a mere sponger who used Vicars' home and friendship to advance his own social and financial interests. It soon became clear that a new assessment must be made.

The first surprise came when Shackleton explained that, during the two years which had elapsed since he and Vicars leased the house, he had spent only two months and two weeks in Dublin. Yet, during the whole period, he had paid half the rent, half the rates and taxes, half the servants' wages, both board and ordinary, and half the laundry bills of all the household linen including sheets. The only household expenses which Vicars had to pay entirely for himself were the washing of his clothes and the cost of his food. The servants were kept on board wages but, when Shackleton was in residence, he paid for half the food consumed. He had also made himself responsible for the total upkeep of the gardens. He also paid for half of all repairs to the house, including the alteration of grates and similar items of expenditure.

'To make certain that I was not using separate food that had been bought the day before I arrived,' Shackleton explained, 'I always counted half of the day previous to my arrival, allowing for the day after I had left.'

This meticulous system of accounting, his seemingly over-generous treatment of Vicars, are very hard to assimilate with the portrait of Shackleton which Goldney had painted in such dark colours. In any case, the Commissioners must have wondered how Vicars could ever have described Shackleton as 'a guest in my house'.

'May I ask you, Mr Shackleton,' asked the Chairman, 'are you well off?'

'Well, it depends on what you call well-off. I have enough to live on.'

Another of the Commissioners, Mr Starkie, was still puzzled.

'Were you paying accommodation elsewhere at the time?'

'Yes,' replied Shackleton. 'I had a flat in Park Lane.'

More baffled than ever, the Chairman moved on to other topics.

'While you were living in the house, you were well acquainted with Sir Arthur Vicars' habits?'

Shackleton agreed. Then, answering further questions, he said that only twice, on Sundays, had Vicars lent him his latch-key to the front door of the Office that he might collect any letters which might have come for him. He had never held at any time either the key to the strong-room or the key to the safe.

'Were you in monetary difficulties in 1907?'

'Yes,' said Shackleton without the least hesitation. 'Well, I had been for two years, I may say, in difficulties; that is to say, my difficulties could easily have been relieved had I chosen to go to my family and tell them, but for various reasons I did not care to do so; and I borrowed money, not from my banker, but from a money-lender. You may ask any questions you like, but I understood it was merely in relation to Sir Arthur Vicars and the custody of the keys that I was to come here. But I am quite prepared to answer any questions.'

He was then asked about the bills which Goldney had mentioned. Again with complete frankness he began to tell the Commissioners what they wished to know. Then, apparently for the first time, he noticed a shorthand-writer taking down all that was said.

'The sums were – one was for £650.' There he broke off. Then he asked a question. 'None of this will appear in the Press?'

'This will be taken down,' he was told.

'But I do not mind a bit so long as it does not appear in the Press. It would be very unpleasant to me if these things came out.'

'I must warn you before you go any further,' the Chairman told him. 'It will be printed, and it may be published.'

Shackleton was, not unreasonably, annoyed at this.

'Then I consider that I should have been told of this beforehand, I do not mean it disrespectfully, but I think it is rather unfair that I should have been allowed to make these statements, because it is a serious matter in business. . . . I was given to understand that the investigation was private. It has been stated in the papers that it is private.'

The Chairman did his best to explain.

'It is private in this sense, that the public are not present here; but the evidence is being taken down and will be printed, and may be published.'

'Then I think that that statement should have been given to me before. My reason is this, that it would be very injurious to me in business, were it known that, at a period when I was engaged in a rather large business transaction, I was absolutely in monetary difficulties to any extent.'

Having made his protest, Shackleton accepted the situation without further demur. He gave the fullest explanation about the bills which Goldney and Vicars had backed for him. Nothing was said to him about the visit he and his 'family solicitor' had paid to Abbots Barton; but Mr Chester Jones asked whether Vicars had obtained any money from these bills. Shackleton told him that Vicars had been paid £100.

'Was that,' asked the Chairman, 'the consideration for his backing the bill for you?'

'I do not know what it was. I do not know what was in his
mind.' Then, after saying that Vicars had asked him to borrow
money for him, which Shackleton did not wish to do, he went
on; 'I may mention at the outset, in defence of myself, that the
first bill which Goldney backed I never had a penny of. It was
to save a friend from being made bankrupt.'

He offered to write down the name of this friend, but the
Commissioners seem to have accepted this extraordinary statement at its face value. There is no doubt that, despite all they
had heard about him, these gentlemen had been uncommonly
impressed by Shackleton. They now asked about the misunderstandings which had led Vicars to believe that Shackleton
knew where the Jewels were. So he told them of his meeting with
Sir Patrick Coll in Harrogate, and of what Sir Patrick told him,
and how he had written at once to Vicars and to young Peirce
Mahony. The Solicitor-General inquired if his letter to Vicars
was of a congratulatory nature.

'I did not write to congratulate,' replied Shackleton. 'I wrote
rather angrily that I had not been told that the Jewels were
recovered.'

It was soon after he had written this letter that he met Goldney in London to discuss their financial business. From that
meeting Goldney had gone hot-foot to Scotland Yard to accuse
Shackleton of knowing where the Jewels were. Since that time,
Shackleton told the Commissioners, both Vicars and Goldney
had left no stone unturned to denigrate his character.

It had been after that that Vicars had written to Shackleton
from Abbots Barton:

> My dear F.,
> Frank tells me you are going to fix up everything for
> him and me on Tuesday, or one day this week.
> This being so, I am giving Frank a sum of £250 to give
> you from me through his solicitor, Sir George Lewis, in
> payment of the sums you advanced to me for changing
> houses and for additional expenses for our joint house
> and household, etc.
> I note you claim £300, but as there are sundry out-
> standing accounts due. . . .
> Sir George Lewis will hand you the £250 when you

hand over to him the two cancelled bills of £600 and £750. Now that you evidently know the whereabouts of the Jewels, from what you said to both Frank and me, I hope you have told Mr Kane everything calculated to facilitate matters.

Yours in haste,
A. Vicars, Ulster.

The Solicitor-General now took a slightly tougher line than he had previously. He wished to hear about Shackleton's departure from Dublin on the 6th or 7th of June. Then he asked about his return to Ireland.

'I came over here on Monday, 8th July, having seen Mr Kane at Scotland Yard in the afternoon.'

'Did you ever stay at the London and North Western Hotel at North Wall?'

'Never!'

'If it were suggested that you had stayed there and not gone to Sir Arthur Vicars?'

'Not true!'

Shackleton then said that the police had already checked very thoroughly his account of his movements while he had been in England, and he understood that they were completely satisfied.

(This story about Shackleton having stayed at the somewhat seedy hotel on the North Wall was, it will be remembered, mentioned by Vicars to Detective Kerr. This might have been the information given to Vicars by Mr McEnnery; but, since the story had been investigated and found untrue, it is not clear why the subject was dragged up at this juncture.)

Now it was Shackleton's prophetic remark at Lady Ormonde's luncheon party that occupied the attention of the Commissioners.

'Why did you think the Jewels were unsafe?'

'Well, for many reasons. I considered there were too many keys of the door – of the outer door.'

Asked whether he could have taken impressions of the keys while Vicars was in his bath, Shackleton again exhibited that engaging frankness which must always have served him well. He agreed that he could have done so.

'I don't say,' he went on, 'that I was always going into his room, because he used to grumble that I got up so early. He said that I was like a Donegal peasant getting up at cock-crow; but I used to go to bed early, which was one of his grievances, because he had no companion.'

The Chairman next explained that Vicars had lost a key and did not recover it until after Shackleton's return to Dublin, when he found it on his dressing-table.

'The key of his office?' asked Shackleton.

'No, of the outer door. Did you take that latch-key?'

'I did not, sir. I never heard of it.'

Once more the trend of questioning was given a new twist. Shackleton was asked further questions about the bills which Goldney had signed, and about the termination of the arrangements made between himself and Vicars with regard to the house in St James's Terrace.

He explained that he had been able to arrange the cancellation of the bills backed by Goldney and Vicars by selling shares. The Chairman then told him that the Commissioners had been told that Sir George Lewis had had to bring considerable pressure to bear before Shackleton had produced the money to cancel the bills. Was there any truth in that statement?

'Absolutely none,' declared the witness. 'I had extreme difficulty in getting my money from Sir George Lewis.'

He explained that, despite Vicars' promise, at least a week had passed, after he had returned the cancelled bills, before Lewis sent him the £250. The lawyer had hoped by these delaying tactics to obtain Shackleton's signature to a full discharge of any further claims he might have against Vicars; and this, very reasonably, Shackleton had refused to give.

As to Major Vicars' request that he should terminate his co-tenancy of the house in St James's Terrace, that had been no more than an empty, hurtful gesture. After Shackleton withdrew from the arrangement, the owner of the house had written to tell him that she had been unable to obtain any rent from Vicars. So, in order to help her, Shackleton had resumed his payments.

Then, after Shackleton gave to the Commissioners his version of what had happened at the *séance* and of the misunderstandings which had followed the Bullock Websters' incursion into the affair, his examination was brought to an end. It had taken a long time, but he had made a considerable impression upon his audience. In the report they were to submit to the Lord-Lieutenant, the Commissioners were to write:

> Although it was no part of our duty under Your Excellency's Warrant to conduct a criminal investigation into the robbery of the Jewels, or to take evidence with a view to the ascertainment of the thief, yet as, on the evidence given before us, and now in print, it appears that the name of Mr Francis Richard Shackleton was more than once named as that of the probable or possible author of this great crime, we think it only due to that gentleman to say that he came from San Remo at great inconvenience to give evidence before us, and that there was no evidence whatever before us which would support the suggestion that he was the person who stole the Jewels.

We would like to think that the Commissioners awarded this unsolicited tribute to Shackleton as some slight recompense for what happened to him as soon as he left the library after giving his evidence. No reference to this sequel appears in the Commissioners' report; nor does any word of it seem to have reached the journalists who wrote so much about the Inquiry. Only the *Gaelic-American*, of 4th July, 1908, reported the incident.

> Mr Shackleton [the paper tells us] was examined before the Commission of Inquiry. As he passed from the office where the Commission sat he was taken possession of by a detective and led into another part of the Castle, where Mr William V. Harrel, M.V.O., the Assistant Commissioner of the Dublin Metropolitan Police, was holding a secret inquiry. Here Mr Shackleton's whole private life was turned inside out – evidence of his disgusting misconduct was dragged to light, and after having been cross-examined by the detectives at great length, he was let go with the admonition to leave the country as quickly as possible.

2

As soon as the Inquiry was at an end the Commissioners, with great care and a certain amount of misunderstanding, prepared their Report. Their verdict was the only one they could be expected to find after Vicars and his Counsel had left the library. With the Government determined to justify to the public their dismissal of the King of Arms, and with only their side of the picture being presented to the Commissioners, there was never any hope that Vicars would be vindicated. The crucial passage reads:

> Having fully investigated all the circumstances connected with the loss of the Regalia of the Order of St Patrick, and having examined and considered carefully the arrangements of the Office of Arms in which the Regalia was deposited, and the provisions made by Sir Arthur Vicars, or under his direction, for their safe-keeping, and having regard especially to the inactivity of Sir Arthur Vicars, on the occasion immediately preceding the disappearance of the Jewels, when he knew that the Office and the Strong Room had been opened at night by an unauthorised person, we feel bound to report to Your Excellency that, in our opinion, Sir Arthur Vicars did not exercise due vigilance or proper care as the custodian of the Regalia.

The chief points upon which, it appears to us, the Commissioners reached conclusions based upon insufficient evidence are these. In Para. 13 of the Report it is stated that:

> Sir Arthur Vicars told Sergeant Sheehan on the 20th of September that his own latch key had been lost on the previous 28th June, and that he did not recover it until the 9th or 10th July, when it was found on his dressing-table.

Yet, in his evidence, Kerr had stated that, on the Monday after the discovery of the theft – that is, on 8th July, the day upon which Shackleton travelled up from Penshurst to London – Vicars had in his possession two keys to the outer door of the Office of Arms; and of these '*Kerr believed*' Ulster has said to him:

> This is one that I got from Mr Mahony, and this is another one that I mislaid. I discovered that this morning.

This must clear Shackleton of any continuing suggestion that it was he who, after his return to Dublin, placed the missing key upon Ulster's dressing-table.

Again, although the Commissioners had listened to much irrelevant evidence, several points of obvious importance were ignored completely. No questions were asked, for instance, regarding the choice and suitability of the Bedford Tower as a place of security for objects as valuable as were the Crown Jewels of Ireland. Again, though much was said of Vicars' negligence in failing to insist that the safe should be placed in the strong-room, no one pointed out that, once he and Sir George Holmes had agreed that the regalia should remain in the safe until the Board of Works might provide a smaller one, it would have been much wiser if the existing safe had been taken upstairs and placed in Vicars' private office rather than left in the library.

We have already mentioned the complete lack of information given about the military and police guards on duty outside the Office of Arms. Even Kerr's nightly inspection was questioned only in the most superficial manner. It might have been thought that the Commissioners would regard his routine searches as very unsatisfactory. His nightly tour of the rooms in the Bedford Tower was at an end by half-past seven or eight o'clock, and Kerr never returned to make a surprise check. His statement that he examined every room each time he inspected the building was never questioned, although such routine checks are notoriously liable to curtailment. Since the police were responsible for the safety of the contents of the Bedford Tower when the staff was absent from the building, it might have been thought that an officer would be stationed within the Office of Arms throughout the night. That these aspects of the security arrangements seem never to have been considered by the Commissioners leaves us with the unfortunate impression that they were chiefly interested in confirming the Government's decision, already taken, that Vicars must go.

3

On 30th January Sir James Dougherty sent the following letter to Vicars.

Referring to my letter of the 23rd October last I am directed by the Lords Justices to state that Letters Patent have this day passed the Great Seal of Ireland revoking the Letters Patent constituting you Ulster King of Arms, and appointing a successor to you in that office.

I am to inform you that, by direction of Their Excellencies, the Office of Arms will be closed tomorrow (Friday), and I am to request you to arrange, either by attendance at the office, or otherwise, as may be most convenient to you, to hand over to your successor the keys belonging to the Office and the Crown Property in your custody, at 12 o'clock on Saturday next, the 1st February.

Vicars immediately sent a copy of this letter to the Irish press, and this appeared in the same issue as did the Report of the Commissioners. At the same time Vicars forwarded the following statement to the newspapers.

Sir,

Owing to an attack of bronchitis I have not been at my office since Monday last. Late yesterday evening I received a letter from the Assistant Under-Secretary, of which I enclose a copy.

My clerk, on presenting himself to-day at the office, was refused admission.

On October 23rd I received an intimation from the Assistant Under-Secretary that I was to be relieved of my office, but giving no reasons.

In answer to my demand for an inquiry I received a reply from the Assistant Under-Secretary in the following terms:

With regard to your request for an inquiry in your letter of the 25th inst., I am to state that His Excellency is advised that your office has been legally and properly terminated, and I am, therefore, to inform you that your request for an inquiry cannot be complied with.

I was subsequently asked more than once to tender my resignation, and suggestions were even made regarding a pension. All these offers I have indignantly refused and have repeatedly demanded a full public and judicial inquiry into all the circumstances.

On December 7th, 1907, His Excellency wrote to my brother Mr Peirce O'Mahony that, unless I sent in my resignation by Monday evening, December 9th, my office would be declared vacant in the *Gazette* of Tuesday December 10th.

On these various changes of position on the part of the Irish Government it is unnecessary to comment.

Seeing that I have never yet been informed definitely of the charges against me, though I have frequently demanded that they should be formulated, and that I should be given an opportunity of meeting my accusers in the light of day before a public and judicial tribunal, it seems to be little short of scandalous that the Irish Government should thus summarily and with such indecent haste dismiss me after fifteen years' faithful service. That they should do so, however, in the face of the demand, coming from all classes, without distinction of politics, for a public and judicial inquiry seems to show a desire to avoid publicity which I, at least, do not share.

As an Irishman by family and birth I appeal to my fellow countrymen to demand for me the right to be judged in public by an impartial tribunal, a right which those now responsible for the government of this country have hitherto denied me. It is true I am only a private individual, and have never taken part in any political matters, but a Government that denies to even the humblest subject that most elementary right of a free people – namely, to meet his accusers in the light of day – strikes at the root of all freedom, and if allowed to persist in its reckless course will deprive us of those liberties which are supposed to be guaranteed to us by the Constitution.

I am (etc.).

At the conclusion of a further statement by Peirce O'Mahony, which appeared at the same time, is this somewhat ambiguous tribute:

The Commissioners appear to have performed their allotted task to the best of their ability, and have placed the Irish Government under a great obligation.

As foretold by Dougherty, a typewritten notice was affixed to the door of the Office of Arms on 31st January, announcing that the building would be closed until noon on the following day. But, though the newly appointed Ulster waited for his predecessor to call upon him, he waited in vain. Neither then nor at any future time did Arthur Vicars return to the Bedford Tower.

The appointment of the new Ulster King of Arms is said to have had a curious genesis. At a meeting of the Privy Council, presided over by the King, it was reported that two members of the College of Arms in London had declined to consider the possibility of succeeding Vicars in Dublin. There appeared to be no other candidate; but the King was insistent that one must be found. In their dilemma the Earl of Pembroke, a Privy Councillor and the largest single landlord in Dublin, proposed the name of his son-in-law, Captain Nevile Rodwell Wilkinson, Coldstream Guards, who was then living at Mount Merrion, Lord Pembroke's home in Ireland. King Edward was delighted; and, when one Privy Councillor ventured to ask if Captain Wilkinson[1] knew anything about heraldry, His Majesty swept such considerations aside.

'That doesn't matter,' he declared, 'so long as he's honest.'

For Vicars, the announcement in the *Gazette* was a shattering blow. His make-believe world, with its gilt crown and its tabards, its heraldic beasts and mediaeval phraseology, fell in ruins about him. Also, his financial position was, to say the least of it, precarious.

It was now that Peirce O'Mahony displayed the generosity and understanding he had always shown to those whom he regarded as the victims of persecution. With his elder brother George, he offered Vicars a home, whether at Grange Con or Kilmorna, where he might recover his self-respect and peace of mind. Not yet, however, was Vicars to be allowed to re-shape his memories in such a way that recent events would appear to be no more than a temporary set-back. On the very day that Captain Wilkinson assumed office, the *Gaelic-American* devoted its leading article to the Irish Crown Jewels. Until now the paper had paid little attention to the measures taken with a view to obtaining a public inquiry into the theft of the regalia; and it is clear that its opinions had been formed on the recommendations of Arthur Griffith and his friends. At this point, however, it was decided to concentrate upon one particular matter in order to goad Lord Aberdeen.

> It was perfectly obvious from the start [declared the leader-writer] that the Commission ordered by that paragon of virtue, King Edward, to inquire into the disappearance of the Dublin Castle State Jewels, was intended not to discover and expose

[1] He was to be the last Ulster King of Arms, the office lapsing at his death in 1940. During his tenure, he left all questions of heraldry and genealogy to his deputies, Mr Burtchaell and Mr Thomas U. Sadleir; but he collected the objects of heraldic interest now shown in the library of the Office of Arms. In 1943 his functions passed to the Chief Herald for Ireland.

the thief, but to cover his tracks and screen him. While the rotten Dublin and London press was trying to make the public believe that King Edward was determined to have the most open and complete inquiry into the affair, the Commission proceeded to conduct its inquiry in the strictest secrecy and so openly showed the influences that it was acting under, that Sir Arthur Vicars, Ulster King of Arms, who was the official charged with the custody of the jewels, and his counsel withdrew from the proceedings.

Then, after saying that Mr Campbell's action had alarmed the 'creatures of the Castle Ring who sat on the Commission', the writer quoted at length the letter written by Vicars' lawyers in reply to the Commissioners' urgent invitation that Vicars and his Counsel would reconsider their decision. The article continues:

> The Dublin Castle Ring and its principals at the Vice-regal Lodge and the Irish Office in London will not and cannot agree to this [a public inquiry] for it would mean the laying bare of the loathsome character of English rule in Ireland and the exposure of the vermin that flourish on it. As to the West British Imperialistic Parliamentarians, we look for nothing from them. . . . They are all too interested in maintaining existing conditions, and if the work of clearing out the rogues that infest Dublin Castle and purifying the moral and political atmosphere that emanates from it is ever to be done, it must be done by the Irish people themselves. They, and they alone, can do it.

It was not only the Irish Americans who saw their chance of baiting the British Government, for there was a continuing spate of criticism in the English papers. A new theory was put forward by the *Pall Mall Gazette* in the following terms:

> The jewels were not abstracted for any nefarious purpose, and they have not been broken up at all. In other words the abstraction of the jewels is attributable to some obscure motive of revenge against Sir Arthur Vicars or some other person or persons, and a belief is held . . . that the jewels have been hidden, and that with due vigilance they may be recovered.
> . . . It seems certain that the Dublin police have shown a singular disinclination to follow up an obvious clue, and that they have leaned towards a view of the case which the known facts would seem to show is erroneous.

... The point then is, who had access to Sir Arthur Vicars'
key? And if there is a person known to have had access to the
key, who is he and where is he?

More was to be heard later concerning this theory of revenge;
and it seems probable that the writer knew something of the
story told by Peirce O'Mahony to his guests at Grange Con.

Then, on 28th February, Miss Marie Corelli published her
shocked denunciation of clairvoyance. After pouring scorn upon
Vicars and Shackleton, she turned her attention to the official
circle at Dublin Castle, declaiming against

the scandalous screening of a thief by Government orders. For
in no other way can it be regarded, seeing that the Lord Lieutenant of Ireland and the Chief Secretary are apparently lending themselves to a policy of silence respecting a robbery of
national jewels.

One would have thought that Lord Aberdeen would have
left no stone unturned in the pursuit of a thief who had taken
the country's property during his term of office; and that even
as a gentleman, apart from his position of authority, he would
not have rested till he had established the position of Sir Arthur
Vicars on a more comprehensive footing of honour. But he
takes the matter with such an astounding coolness that it would
seem he conceives thieving no robbery. . . . If England's regalia
had been stolen there would be such a hue and cry as has perhaps never been seen or known. Ireland may be robbed by
protected 'pickers and stealers' and 'No further search will be
made'. And if Irish folk feel any desire to protest against this
arbitrary settlement – 'no notice is to be taken of any demand
for a public inquiry from any quarter whatsoever'.

Under the special and particular protection of law and
Government, therefore, thieving may now become the
fashionable new pastime of the Upper Ten as a kind of off-
shoot of 'Bridge'. The news that 'No further search will be
made' for the Dublin Crown Jewels must be balm to the souls
of those smart gentlefolk who may be meditating depredations
on other people's property. Care must be taken, however,
to remember that only persons of the nobility and gentry are
likely to be eligible for the Government licence to steal. Low-
class thieves will go to prison as usual.

Her nonsense would not be worth resurrecting were it not
that it drew from Peirce O'Mahony yet another statement in

his brother's defence, which he prefaced by a somewhat wry tribute to Miss Corelli, his 'homage to her brilliant and noble courage'.

I have openly stated my belief [he wrote] that the Commission was packed by the Castle to obtain a verdict in its own favour, and that the present Attorney-General for Ireland stated in the House on February 4th that an official of Dublin Castle had urged him to pollute the 'Fountain of Justice' by packing a jury in order to obtain a verdict. It is therefore not hard to believe that the same official would without hesitation pack a commission to whitewash and shield his superiors. . . .

The robbery was discovered on July 6th, and for months friendly communications passed between my brother and the authorities. . . . Suddenly, in October, my brother became aware that a secret inquiry was going on behind his back, and on October 23rd he was informed that his office 'had been legally and properly terminated'. . . . From that day to this I have never ceased to work for the vindication of my brother's character from the stain sought to be cast upon it by this Minister of the Crown, who seems to be absolutely devoid of what are supposed to be the feelings of an English gentleman.

At any rate I have openly accused the Chief Secretary of conduct unworthy of a gentleman; I have brought the accusation before the Speaker of the House of Commons, once called the finest club in Europe; I have brought it under the notice of His Majesty the King. The Right Hon. A. Birrell has taken it lying down, because he knows that if he challenges me in public court, I will drive the accusation home, vindicate to the full the honour of my brother and expose the corruption and rottenness of Dublin Castle officialdom, over which he so honourably presides. I have accused the police of wilfully withholding evidence in their possession that is favourable to my brother. I . . . now go further, and I state deliberately that the Government do not wish to find the thief, because one suspected man and one of his associates, also suspected, are known to the police as men of unclean lives, and have threatened to involve Society in an unsavoury scandal; and so, in this twentieth century, under the enlightened rule of the most constitutional monarch in Europe, an official of hitherto unblemished character and name is to be dismissed and ruined and denied the opportunity of meeting his accusers in the open – a right accorded to the meanest criminal – because a few titled members of what are called so falsely the 'Upper Ten' and who

11

circle round the throne, possess characters so absolutely rotten and degraded that they fear to face the threats of two men whom the Rt. Hon. A. Birrell has described as 'abandoned ruffians'. My brother's honour is of no account to them – titled corruption must be shielded from the public gaze. Not thus, however, can they stem the fetid tide.

'One suspected man and one of his associates, also suspected. . . .'

But Shackleton had been cleared of all complicity in the theft, and the name of his associate had never been published in connection with the mystery; for the *Gaelic-American*, it will be remembered, had presented Captain Gorges to its readers as Captain Gaudeans. Not even Peirce O'Mahony, it will be noted, now named the two men he suspected of the crime. This conspiracy of silence, uniting everyone connected with the case, is only explicable if all of them, again including O'Mahony, feared that an open denunciation of Shackleton and Gorges might unleash a spate of revelations which would do no one any good and might well cause incalculable harm to causes and reputations which they held dear.

Despite what the *Gaelic-American* had said of the Irish Members of Parliament, there were a number who never missed an opportunity of raising the subject of the lost regalia in the House of Commons. Birrell, however, always made the same reply. Nothing was known; there was nothing he could tell the House. Nothing, nothing, nothing. . . .

Then, on 1st April, 1908, the Member for Lewisham, Mr Coates, asked if Mr Birrell could state the dates between which the Crown Jewels must have been stolen from Dublin Castle. No one looked for an answer any different from that he had given on so many previous occasions. He stated, to begin with, what we already know: that the Jewels had been taken between 11th June and 6th July.

'As I am on this subject,' he went on, surprisingly, 'I may refer to a most cowardly falsehood connecting the name of Lord Haddo with the theft of the jewels, which has obtained wide circulation both in Dublin and in London, and had found its way into certain newspapers. Ridiculous as such a statement may appear, it is not always easy to maintain total indifference to such charges. (Hear, hear.) I am able to say, of my own knowledge, that Lord Haddo left Dublin on 7th March, 1907, and lived in Scotland and England from that time without intermission until 7th December. I hope this statement may put an end to the business of the scandal-mongers – in this particular at all events. (Loud cheers.) If I may be permitted to mention the name of the Lord-Lieutenant in the matter, I may add that Lord Aberdeen was, from the first, most anxious that there should be the fullest possible inquiry into all the circumstances attending the loss of the Crown Jewels, and would have been glad if it had been possible to call into existence a statutory commission for that purpose.' (Cheers.)

This statement, which throws such an entirely new light upon the Lord-Lieutenant's feelings, was allowed to pass unchallenged; but the Member for North Armagh, Mr Moore, rose at once to ask a supplementary question.

'Arising out of that and fully accepting the disclaimer on the part of Lord Haddo (Cries of 'Oh!'), will the right hon. gentleman take equal steps for the prevention of scandal-mongering and insinuations against Lord Ashtown, who has been equally unfairly abused?' (Hear, hear.)

The Speaker, after calling for order, held that Mr Moore's inquiry did not arise out of the preceding question. Redmond then asked Mr Birrell if it was true that Dublin Herald and Athlone Pursuivant were asked to resign before the appointment of the Commission and, if so, why that was done. Birrell, however, would not be drawn, saying that he must have notice of that question. Then the Member for Donegal, Mr MacNeill, rose to ask a further question.

'Inasmuch as the libels to which the right hon. gentleman has referred have been published in England, may I ask him why have no proceedings been taken for criminal libel in the criminal courts?'

'I can only say,' replied Birrell, 'that legal advice has been taken on the matter, and action, or rather inaction, has been adopted in accordance with that advice.'

This decision did nothing to extinguish the gossip to which Birrell had referred; but, though the *Gaelic-American* seized on the Irish Secretary's statement to make another scathing attack upon the Government in the issue of 11th April, no one appears to have appreciated the new light which the Parliamentary statement throws upon the evidence given by Mrs Farrell before the Commission of Inquiry.

It will be remembered that the office cleaner had said that she had seen 'the strange gentleman' in the library 'in the spring – some five or six months earlier'; that is, presumably, in the January or February of 1907. So, although Lord Haddo had a perfect and complete alibi for the period during which the regalia was taken, Birrell's statement that the Lord-Lieutenant's son had left Ireland on 7th March does nothing to demolish Mrs Farrell's belief that the early morning visitor she had seen in the Office of Arms was Lord Haddo. The decision of the authorities not to investigate fully Mrs Farrell's story, and to make their findings public, was foolish in the extreme. It led to the birth of the ridiculous legend, still widely held, that Lord Haddo was in some way implicated in the disappearance of the Jewels.

Throughout this period Vicars must have suffered agonies of embarrassment and mental discomfort. He had refused the pension offered by the Government, but his financial position was extremely precarious. His beloved books, including those he had lent to the Office of Arms, were sold at Sothebys during 1908, as was his collection of book-plates, probably one of the finest formed at that period; but these sales brought a total of no more than £778 12s. 6d. This was certainly not sufficient to keep him in the way of life to which he had long been accustomed. Nevertheless, despite his difficulties, Vicars still hoped to create for himself a new life and to obtain a reversal of the findings of the Commission of Inquiry.

Then, in June, 1908, as interest in the case was dwindling, it was sharply revived by the activities of an eccentric barrister, John Wallace. This pertinacious Don Quixote opened his campaign by applying, in the King's Bench Division in Dublin, for warrants for the arrest of Lord Aberdeen and Mr Birrell on charges of having conspired together to steal the Crown Jewels and accuse Vicars of the theft in order to install a man of their own choice in his place. When this application, not altogether surprisingly, failed, Mr Wallace did not give up. In December he appeared before the Chief Baron and asked for a warrant for the arrest of Peirce Mahony, Cork Herald. When this also was refused, Wallace charged the Chief Baron and Mr Justice Andrews with perjury. Still, however, Vicars' champion would not accept defeat. Even as late as 14th July, 1914, he appeared in the Southern Police Court in Dublin, asking for warrants for the arrest of Sir John Ross of Bladensburg 'for being the chief manual in bringing the Crown Jewels in their cases to where Lord Aberdeen was lying in wait'.

So, on this characteristically British note of lofty and muddled eccentricity, the fate of the Irish Crown Jewels faded for the time being from the public interest.

BOOK FIVE

The Aftermath

CHAPTER ONE

Although the case was regarded officially as closed, it remained for many of those concerned in it as a marchstone, from which their several paths ran down to disaster and to death.

For Peirce Mahony, however, life continued very much as it had done before the robbery. It will be remembered that Lord Aberdeen had told Lord Knollys that he had asked for the resignations of Vicars, Shackleton, Goldney and Mahony; but Mahony remained, apparently without a break, as Cork Herald. Possibly the Irish authorities were less realistic than King Edward and fondly believed that no married man could be interested in sodomy. The attitude of officialdom is less interesting than is Mahony's decision to hold office after the dismissal of his uncle and at the same time that his father was inveighing publicly and in private against the King, the Lord-Lieutenant and the Irish Secretary. Certainly Mahony had retained the post from 1905 despite his father's marked disapproval; but that dispute had been a private matter between his father, his uncle and himself. Now, with everything connected with the Office of Arms given the maximum publicity, Mahony apparently found no added difficulty in continuing to serve as Cork Herald. It would seem that he, like his uncle, possessed the ability to ignore anything he did not wish to recognise. Or perhaps he was endowed with the obstinacy of a weak man.

As with so many first-born sons of men with vivid personalities, Peirce Mahony showed none of those qualities which made his father so remarkable. He moves like a shadow through the story, a handsome extra with scarcely a line to speak. Yet, perhaps because of the oddly nebulous impression he leaves with us, his story bristles with unanswered questions.

Whether or not his quarrel with his father survived the *rapprochement* between Peirce O'Mahony and Vicars, it was certainly healed by 1910, the year which saw him resign from the Office of Arms and take his call to the bar by King's Inn, Dublin. For Peirce Mahony then left Dublin and moved to a house belonging to his father.

Kilmurray House on Castle Island, County Kerry, is a Georgian house with white-painted walls and spacious windows which reflect every mutation of light and shade in the ever-changing Irish sky. Here, from time to time, came Mrs Mahony's sister, Gertrude Wright, and here, a frequent visitor, came Arthur Vicars from nearby Kilmorna. This was, for all of them, an almost idyllic period in which even Vicars found it possible, for a time, to forget his wrongs. Even in the summer of 1914, when Ireland trembled on the brink of civil war and the newspapers were filled with stories of growing tension in Europe, it was difficult for those on Castle Island to believe that anything could possibly destroy the peace which enclosed them.

In mid-July, however, came the first disturbing move. The persistent Mr Wallace had appeared in Dublin and was demanding the arrest of Lord Aberdeen and Sir John Ross. Although we do not know upon what grounds this barrister had once sought the issue of a writ against Peirce Mahony, the latter can scarcely have failed to wonder if Mr Wallace's new campaign against the entrenched authority of Dublin Castle would bring trouble of one kind or another to him. But even if this cloud upon the horizon was no larger than the Red Hand of Ulster on a baronet's shield, the immediate future darkened materially when Peirce Mahony was summoned to Grange Con.

Probably there had never been over-much sympathy between this father and son; but, in this present juncture of world affairs, Peirce O'Mahony must have felt that there were topics he must discuss with his elder son. In the event of Russia becoming involved in even a limited European war, O'Mahony's fortune in that country might well be threatened. Besides, the older man viewed the immediate prospect with sadness, for it seemed inevitable that this conflict would be fought out in those Balkan countries with which he had so strong an affinity. Not this time would he be able to offer sanctuary to war refugees in Ireland, for that country was moving swiftly towards seemingly unavoidable civil strife. So staunch a Nationalist as Peirce O'Mahony must have known of the plans, then taking shape, by which the leaders of that party were preparing to bring arms into Southern Ireland in order to counter the similar methods being practised by the Unionists in the North. In Ulster, Carson's importation of arms had met with no interference from the Government, and his men marched and drilled openly. No one could tell, however, how the authorities in Dublin would react to similar action by their opponents in the South. Some 900 rifles and 29,000 rounds of ammunition were to be landed at Howth on Sunday, 27th July; and those like Peirce O'Mahony, who had seen his hopes for Ireland so often extinguished, viewed the immediate future with the greatest anxiety. At this time, when they were faced with crisis interwoven with crisis, O'Mahony sent for his son; but it is doubtful whether they were brought any closer to each other.

In the atmosphere of impending doom and heightening tension which reigned at Grange Con, it must have been with a sense of heartening relief that Peirce Mahony received an invitation to join some neighbours for tea on the Saturday afternoon preceding that fatal Sunday. He was to row across the lake to meet them and, before he left the house, he went to the gun-room and selected a double-barrelled gun and some ammunition. The lake was thronged with water-fowl; and, though the season had not yet opened, that was not a consideration likely to deter a Mahony while upon the surface of his father's lake.

Not until the following day was it realised that Peirce Mahony had neither joined his friends nor returned to Grange Con. A search was at once instituted, but it was afternoon before Athanas Blagoff, one of O'Mahony's Bulgarian protégés, found young Mahony's body lying in the lake near the boathouse. He dragged the body from the water and was about to start artificial respiration when he saw there was blood upon Mahony's clothes. Peirce had been shot through the heart.

Later investigations were to show that Mahony had not taken the key of the boathouse when he went down to the lake; so, as the boathouse was locked, he would have had to climb over a low barbed wire fence to reach the boat. Since both barrels of the gun had been fired, it was supposed that, having negotiated the wire and entered the boat, experienced sportsman though he was, he proceeded to draw the gun over the fence, its barrels pointing towards his heart. Marks on the triggers were said to have been caused by a loose strand of wire that was discovered on the fence. As the double charge entered Mahony's heart, he had toppled out of the boat into the lake. At the inquest, medical evidence was given to the effect that the wounds could not have been intentionally self-inflicted; and the jury found that the deceased had been accidentally shot and that no blame attached to anyone.[1]

The tragedy received no more than a brief notice in the Irish Press, which was filled with accounts of the successful gun-running that took place according to schedule at Howth that Sunday morning, and of the tragedy which followed. Troops were sent to disperse the Nationalist Volunteers and succeeded in doing so, though they found very few of the smuggled arms. As a detachment of Scottish Borderers were returning to their quarters they met a menacing crowd of Dubliners and, as they turned into Bachelor's Walk, their way was barred to them. In the confusion which followed, shots were fired. Two men and one woman were killed, thirty-two persons were wounded; the first casualties in the renewed struggle for Ireland's freedom.

Throughout that day Sir James Dougherty, a great deal less assured then, when his own future was in the balance, than when Arthur Vicars had sought for no more than common justice, procrastinated and quibbled, leaving the final decisions to be taken by Mr Harrel. So, in the tortuous aftermath of that day's shooting, when Lord Aberdeen and his Government had once more to choose a scapegoat to bear the stigma of their own inadequacies, their choice fell upon Harrel, a man of honour and character deserving of better masters. Thus did the wheel turn full circle; and the man who had once ordered Shackleton to leave Ireland, was himself dismissed from office.

Forty years later, and Ireland's freedom won, we are able to survey what little is known of Peirce Mahony's death; and we confess that we find it difficult to accept the verdict of the jury. Did that medical witness really believe that, had he wished to do so, Peirce Mahony could not have chosen just this way to take his own life? There would seem, after all, no reason why he should not have done intentionally what he probably did by accident.

[1] *Freeman's Journal*, 29th July, 1914.

This is a mystery with no known solution. We are therefore driven to consider every possibility; and we confess that the fact that Peirce Mahony died at this particular juncture leaves us with the uneasy feeling that it must have had some connection with other incidents which occurred about this time. To believe otherwise is to ask almost too much of the long arm of coincidence.

Here are some of the possibilities which occur to us. Did the reappearance of Mr Wallace, seven years after he had applied for a warrant against Peirce Mahony, bring the latter to a point of dilemma from which, to him, death seemed to offer the only escape? Had Kerr been right when he stated that Vicars told him, on the Monday after the discovery of the theft, that he had that day found his lost key upon his dressing-table? Because, if so, it could have been Mahony who placed it there when he was in the house on the Saturday evening.[1] Had it been he who was responsible for introducing the actual thief into the Office of Arms?

If such were the case, it appears to us possible that Peirce Mahony had been induced to play such a part by some form of blackmail or, much more probably, he was tricked into doing so by someone who presented the whole plot as an immense practical joke, similar to, but much more spectacular than, that earlier occasion when one of Vicars' guests had taken his keys and abstracted the jewels from the safe. This would explain, as does nothing else, why Peirce Mahony continued as Cork Herald after his uncle's dismissal. He may have clung to office in the hope that those who had fooled him would, in the end, redeem their promise and return the regalia; and Mahony believed that, by retaining his position at the Office of Arms, he might be able to arrange that their return appeared as mysterious as was their disappearance.

Or was it that during those last weeks of his life, when crisis and tension increased throughout a waiting Ireland, Peirce Mahony learnt the identity of the man responsible for the theft and for his uncle's ruin? And was he murdered as a result of that discovery?

When, in 1908, Sir Arthur Conan Doyle wrote for the *Strand*

[1] It should be noted that Horlock could also have placed the key in Vicars' bedroom when he was in the house on the Sunday.

Magazine the tale entitled *The Bruce-Partington Plans*, it is clear that he had accepted the views of his friend Vicars regarding the loss of the Crown Jewels. It is not difficult to recognise Shackleton in the character of the nefarious Colonel Walter, and Peirce Mahony as the unfortunate Cadogan West. This is evident from one passage, in which Sherlock Holmes is telling Colonel Walter that all is known as to his theft of the naval papers he had stolen for a foreign power.

> 'I can assure you,' said Holmes, 'that every essential is already known. We know that you were pressed for money, that you took an impress of the keys which your brother held, and that you entered into a correspondence with Oberstein [the foreign agent]. . . . We are aware that you were seen and followed by young Cadogan West, who had probably some previous reason to suspect you. . . .'[1]

As a result of his interference Cadogan West was murdered, and his death arranged to look like suicide. Had Sir Arthur Conan Doyle, borrowing a framework of fact to construct a work of fiction, written more truly than he ever guessed? Did something happen in the summer of 1914 which made it necessary for someone connected with the loss of the Crown Jewels to remove the potentially dangerous Mahony from the scene? And did that someone, taking a leaf from the case-book of Sherlock Holmes, stage a murder to appear like a case of suicide?

Probably we shall never know.

---

[1] In *His Last Bow*, by Sir Arthur Conan Doyle (John Murray, London, 1917).

CHAPTER TWO

Among the topics which Peirce Mahony may well have discussed with his father on his last visit to Grange Con was one which appeared in the English papers of 15th July, 1914. This reported that an application had been made that the case pending between Miss Mary Josephine Browne and Sir Ernest Shackleton might be expedited. Counsel for the latter had said that, if the claim was simply to recover the sum of £1,000, his client would settle it at once. He was expecting to leave shortly on an expedition to the Antarctic and was anxious that the case might be settled without delay. As the papers contain no further reference to the matter, it would appear that Miss Browne accepted this offer.

News of the circumstances under which Frank Shackleton left Ireland in 1908 do not seem to have reached the English papers, which published the kindly remarks made about him by Chief Inspector Kane and the Commissioners. Indeed, if anyone was so prejudiced as still to harbour any suspicions regarding him, there were others so deeply convinced of his innocence that they were anxious to do all they could to erase from his memory the unkind things which had been said of him in the course of the Inquiry. Chief among these were Miss Browne and Lord Ronald Sutherland-Gower. Not quite so anxious, perhaps, was Lord Ronald's adopted son, Frank Hird.

Lord Ronald Gower's recovery from his epileptic attack had received a set-back when, in November, 1907, his man of business, Mr Culverwell, had died. Lord Ronald, an artist by nature, had never had to manage his financial affairs; and it appeared to him most fortunate that, at this time, so clever a business man as Shackleton was at hand to advise him what to do for the best. In fact, to save himself unnecessary worry, he gave Shackleton a power of attorney over all his financial concerns.

Miss Browne was equally anxious to do what she could to restore Shackleton's *amour propre*, for it was not until this juncture that she sought his advice as to the management of her modest fortune. He suggested that she could not do better than purchase shares in the Celtic Investment Trust, the company financing the North Mexico Land and Timber Company, on behalf of which he had worked so hard during the past few years. The progress of negotiations about the Mexican properties were slow but not unsatisfactory. Mr Frank Alden, a stockbroker of Throgmorton Street, had sent out an independent valuer to inspect the land upon which Shackleton had obtained an option for his company; and this expert confirmed all the claims made as to the value of the land and timber. In consequence, Mr Alden's firm agreed to underwrite the shares of the company – the nominal capital of which was one million pounds – when these should be offered to the public.

In a letter which Vicars wrote to Mr Fuller in July, 1909, just after returning to Grange Con after a protracted visit to London, he gives a picture of Shackleton's life at that period.

> No one knows how Shackleton gets his money – his own family don't know. He bought since the robbery an £850 Motor Car – & lives in a huge house, beautifully furnished at 29 Palace Court, W. These are facts which you can ascertain without difficulty. He lives in great style. He is wonderfully clever – bamboozles everyone & Kane admits he is very clever & at first entirely threw them off the scent by his cool manner.

All this was unknown to Lord Ronald Gower and Frank Hird when they invited Miss Browne and Shackleton to spend Christmas and the New Year with them at Hammerfield. Miss Browne was there from 23rd December, 1909, until 17th January, 1910; but Shackleton could not leave his business affairs for so long a period. He did, however, contrive to get down to Penshurst on three separate occasions while Miss Browne was there.

It was during one of these visits that Miss Browne happened to mention that she would be shortly receiving a thousand pounds which she had lent to a Mr Devitt, who had recently died in Canada, the loan having been secured on a life insurance policy.

'Whenever you get it,' Shackleton advised her, 'let me have it. I will invest it for you in something good. Don't go lending it again.'

So on St Valentine's Day, after some correspondence had passed between them about this money, Miss Browne sent him a cheque for £1,000, asking him to invest it for her. On 24th April, when he called on her in Tavistock, Miss Browne asked him about this money.

'I have invested it in the Celtic,' he told her; but, when she said she would like to discuss with him her investments generally, Shackleton found the time inconvenient. 'For goodness sake don't ask me now. I am so tired. I shall be down on Wednesday, and I will talk it over with you then.'

But neither on the following Wednesday nor at any other time was Miss Browne to have an opportunity to discuss with the young man she had come to regard as a son the very substantial sums she had paid to him.

Probably Miss Browne's inquiries had been prompted by what Frank Hird had told her. For during the two years during which he had been looking after Lord Ronald Gower's affairs, Shackleton and his friend Mr Garlick, who was chiefly responsible for the management of the Celtic Investment Trust Company, had obtained from Lord Ronald large sums of money and share certificates to a very considerable value. Shackleton had immense faith in the ultimate success of his plans for the North Mexico Land and Timber Company; and he had no doubt that, could he but tide over his present financial difficulties, he and his friends would all benefit substantially. So, in February, 1910, when his account at Cox's Bank was overdrawn to the extent of £40,000 on the security of a guarantee signed by Lord Ronald Gower, and some sixty thousand shares in the City of Monte Video Public Works Corporation belonging to himself, he felt no scruples at paying into his account the cheque entrusted to him by Miss Browne. Nor did he hesitate to embark on an elaborate intrigue by which, though he knew these shares in the Monte Video Public Works Corporation were quite worthless, he disposed of five thousand of these shares in exchange for Lord Ronald Gower's cheque for £5,087 13s. It was this transaction which alarmed Frank Hird, when he heard of it; but Shackleton persuaded him that Mr Garlick was responsible for these financial manoeuvres. Hird said that Shackleton must take the management of his affairs out of Garlick's hands as soon as the Mexican Company was finally launched.

Then, as Shackleton attempted to keep at bay both his credi-

12

tors and friends, King Edward again took a hand in shaping the pattern of this young man's life. His Majesty died on 6th May and, two days later, a creditor of the Monte Video Public Works Corporation obtained judgment against its directors for £5,000. They could not pay and, on 6th July, a petition to wind up the Company was presented. The accounts showed a deficiency of £943,000.

To what extent, if any, Shackleton was concerned in the affairs of this company is not known; but, before its position was made public, he received a shattering blow to all his hopes. Soon after the King's death, Mr Alden, who was later to testify that Shackleton 'had worked very hard in connexion with the company, which had certainly looked like being successful', wrote to tell him that, 'owing to a variety of circumstances, of which the death of King Edward was by no means the least', his firm would not be able to underwrite the shares of the North Mexico Land and Timber Company. There was no time for Shackleton to begin all over again. On 6th August, five days before the balance sheet of the Monte Video Public Works Corporation was published, Shackleton met his own creditors. An official of the Bankruptcy Court estimated that his debts amounted to £84,441 12s. 6d.

After he had been adjudged bankrupt Shackleton was involved in two regrettable scenes. First, he walked over to where poor Miss Browne was sitting with Frank Hird and grinned at them. In consequence Hird waited for him to leave the court and, when Shackleton appeared with his brother and one of his sisters, he ran after them calling them thieves and other opprobrious names. He also wrote a series of libellous postcards to Sir Ernest Shackleton bearing wild accusations against him. The explorer threatened to sue Hird for defamation of character, a prospect which interested Vicars greatly. It is noteworthy that, though Shackleton had never brought together Vicars and Lord Ronald Gower and Mr Hird, these three had now, through their common dislike of Shackleton, struck up an acquaintance.

I hear [Vicars wrote to Mr Fuller] that there is a libel action coming on of Sir E. Shackleton against a man – & the defendant tells me that my affair is bound to come up & that he will help me as far as possible. He promises revelations . . . unless E.S. funks an exposure. . . .

In the event, however, it was Hird who evaded the issue. He sent the following letter to Sir Ernest Shackleton.

> Reference to the post cards which I sent to you and various other persons, I am now satisfied that the statements I made with regard to you are unfounded, and I wish to express my regret and apologies to you for what I did. I undertake that there shall be no repetition of such aspersions for my part.

Meanwhile Shackleton had asked that his renewed public examination might be postponed until the spring. The reason for this appears in Vicars' letter to Mr Fuller of 11th October, 1910:

> Yes, Shackleton took a fine house (bought it) in Park Lane, next door to Lady Grosvenor & Sir Rufus Isaacs, & then suddenly went smash for over £100,000. . . . I believe there will be some startling revelations over the bankruptcy. His examination is put off till 4 May 1911, as S. said he had undergone an operation & had to go abroad for the winter for his health! It is astonishing how operations are rendered suddenly necessary sometimes!

When 4th May came, however, Shackleton failed to appear. Again Vicars reported to Mr Fuller:

> I have heard nothing of Shackleton since he absconded to S. Africa. It is a monstrous job that the Bankruptcy officials let him bolt. He evidently got wind that he was going to be prosecuted.

Yet his creditors were slow to take action. Not until 21st September, 1912, was a warrant issued against him. He was charged with having fraudulently converted to his own use a cheque for £1,000 entrusted to him by Miss Browne.

Meanwhile Shackleton was in Portuguese West Africa, where he was working as the manager of a plantation. He was arrested by the Portuguese police at Hanha on 31st October. From there he was taken to the prison in Benguela to await the arrival of a detective from Scotland Yard. To Shackleton's relief Detective Inspector Cooper, an extraordinary figure with heavy curled moustache and bowler hat, reached Benguela on 9th December.

'I will do anything,' Shackleton told him at their first interview, 'to get out of this place. If I have to remain here much longer I am sure I shall be dead.'

Formalities were reduced to the minimum, and on 22nd December Cooper and his prisoner sailed for England on the s.s. *Grandtully*. Photographs taken of the two men on their arrival in England provide evidence of the toll levied on Shackleton by those weeks he had spent in a Portuguese jail. It is hard to believe that the seedy individual in a cloth cap and mackintosh could ever have captured the heart of anyone.

On 10th January, 1913 – five years to the day after the Commission of Inquiry first met in the Office of Arms – Shackleton appeared before Mr Curtis Bennett but, after merely formal proceedings, was remanded. Dr Henry Shackleton found surety for his son in the sum of £1,000, while the defendant entered into his own recognisances for a similar amount.

When the case came up for hearing on 21st January, Shackleton's activities were presented in an altogether unflattering light. It now appeared that, although Miss Browne was suing for no more than £1,000, he had obtained from her no less than £12,778. Of her small fortune nothing remained in the hands of her bankers but 100 shares in the Tavistock Conservative Club. Later, after several adjournments, new charges were brought against Shackleton and Thomas John Garlick, an accountant of George Street, London, W.C. They were accused of defrauding Miss Browne, and of conspiring to defraud Lord Ronald Gower of £50,000 and his adopted son, Frank Hird, of £6,000.

In view of the evidence there can never have been much doubt as to the verdict. Shackleton was sentenced to fifteen months' imprisonment, and Garlick to nine months. An appeal brought in the following October was dismissed.

Frank Shackleton, endowed with looks and charm of a quality granted to few men, possessing the pertinacity to apply himself to business concerns which must, from their very nature, take years to mature, passes into the anonymous world of prison life, never to appear again under his own name. After his release he lived under a pseudonym, dying as anonymously in the years between the two German wars. Looking back across his aspiring life and his forgotten death, we cannot but be touched by the abiding pity of it all.

CHAPTER THREE

On his father's side Francis Bennett-Goldney was descended from a long line of middle-class Welshmen. These had, in recent generations, been as distinguished by their enthusiasm for pure knowledge as by their earnest Christian zeal. His great-grandfather, the Reverend Lewis Evans, was remarkable for having contrived to serve both God and Mars. Vicar of Froxfield in Wiltshire from 1786 until 1827, he was appointed in 1799 to be the first mathematical master at the Royal Military Academy at Woolwich, a post he retained until 1820. Three years later he became a Fellow of the Royal Society and, shortly afterwards, was elected a Fellow of the Antiquarian Society. Thus did he establish a tradition of interests for several of his descendants. When he was able to turn from his divine and mathematical duties, he contributed articles to the Philosophical Magazine.

His son, Arthur Benoni Evans, D.D., of Oxford, followed closely in his father's footsteps. Appointed Professor of Classics and History at the Royal Military College in 1805, when he was only 24, he resigned in 1822 and later became headmaster of Market Bosworth School. A literary dilettante of varied interests, he published a study of Leicestershire dialect as well as many poems and sermons.

In addition to these activities Dr Evans found time to father two sons. The elder was to become Sir John Evans, the first man to place the study of the ancient British coinage on a scientific basis, as well as being an outstanding authority in the fields of geology and archaeology. He is best remembered today as the father and mentor of Sir Arthur Evans, the explorer and exponent of ancient Crete.

Dr Evans' younger son, Sebastian, was no less busy than his brother and only slightly less distinguished. His inherited interests in religion and the antique drew him on to study the techniques practised by mediaeval craftsmen in various media. As a result he became head of the department of design to Messrs Chance, the well-known firm of stained-glass manufacturers near Birmingham. This, however, was not enough to engage fully his bustling enthusiasm; and he was not so dedicated as were many of his windows. Deeply interested in politics, he edited the Conservative paper in Birmingham, the *Daily Gazette*, from 1867 to 1870. Yet he became a life-long friend of Joseph Chamberlain; for Sebastian Evans possessed a rare genius for friendship, numbering among his intimates such men as Thackeray and Darwin, Huxley and Newman, Matthew Arnold and Ruskin.

In 1868 the degree of LL.D. was conferred upon him and, five years later, he was called to the Bar; but, although he built up a successful practice, he threw it up to become editor of *The People*, a Conservative weekly of which he was one of the founders. Still, however, he found time to follow his artistic bent, examples of his work in oils, water colours and black and white being exhibited at the Royal Academy over a number of years.

These exalted occupations and interests did not blind Dr Evans to worldly considerations, and he chose for his wife the daughter of a Mr Francis Bennett-Goldney, a founder and director of the London and Joint Stock Bank. Their marriage was blessed with two sons; Sebastian, of whom we know nothing, and Francis who was destined to become Mayor of Canterbury and Athlone Pursuivant.

It might be expected that Dr Evans would hold unusual views on education, but he certainly broke new ground in that belaboured field when he elected that Francis should be schooled at Bournemouth and in Paris. It was hoped the boy would enter the diplomatic service; but he seems never to have entered any of the professions except that, for a short time, he held a commission in the 6th Battalion, Middlesex Regiment (Militia). Then, when he was twenty-seven, in conformity with the will of one of his mother's family, he relinquished the name of Evans and adopted instead that of Bennett-Goldney. Armed with a double-barrelled name and the fortune that accompanied it, Frank set out to carve for himself a place in the world.

Although he possessed his family's traditional interest in antiquities, he lacked that brilliant critical faculty which distinguished his uncle and cousin. Not for Goldney the narrow field of the scholarly specialist, but rather the broad horizons of an acquisitive 'all-rounder'. With characteristic modesty he was later to describe himself as an authority on Chinese ceramics, Lambeth ware, miniatures and Roman and Saxon relics.

He also found time to write on such diversified subjects as history, art, furniture, decoration and kindred topics.

Frank Goldney had also inherited much of his father's boundless energy. He found time to practise his favourite recreations of riding, swimming and fencing, accomplishments which ensured that, while prosecuting his ambitions and forming his collections, he should not allow himself to deteriorate physically. In the Edwardian manner, Frank Goldney was a fine figure of a man.

By what transitions he arrived with his mother at Goodnestone in Kent we do not know; but they were settled there towards the end of the last century. It was at Goodnestone that Goldney came to the decision that he would conquer Kent; and in 1898 he made the first move towards impressing upon the people of Canterbury the benevolence, the generosity and wide cultural interests he could place at their disposal.

The Beaney Institute and Museum were then being built in Canterbury. So Goldney offered to lend to the Museum a large part of his collections, thus hoping to make use of objects he had acquired which, by their very nature, were not easy to display in a private house. Flint arrow-heads, Roman tear-bottles and fragments of Lambeth pottery can, in the mass, add little to the gaiety of a room.

The committee of the Institute, faced with bare walls and empty cabinets, accepted the offer gratefully; and, almost before these gentlemen were aware of what was happening, Goldney had obtained for himself the post of Honorary Director and Curator of the Institute, a position he was careful to see should be, to all intents and purposes, independent of the Committee. Thus it was that, in March, 1899, without reference to the governing body, he appointed Mr H. T. Mead to be assistant librarian to the Institute at a salary of £100 a year. The Committee, faced with this *fait accompli*, meekly confirmed the appointment.

Possibly this easy victory encouraged Goldney in his ambitious dreams. He now removed to Canterbury, where he obtained from the daughters of a deceased general the lease of their mid-nineteenth century home, Westfield House, which stood in spacious and well-planned grounds. The name did not appeal to Goldney's taste and he renamed that comfortable but undistinguished house Abbots Barton, invoking the picture of some ancient grange nestling almost within the shadow of the great cathedral.

His election to the town council in November, 1902, was but the first step towards a much more exalted goal. Three years later he was elected mayor and, not long afterwards, became an alderman, chosen in preference to several others possessing more valid claims. There can be no doubt that he possessed both charm and ability because, despite the gossip which must have been generated by his resignation of the post of Athlone Pursuivant, he continued as Mayor of Canterbury until 1911.

Despite his unfortunate experience in Dublin, Goldney felt that the House of Commons would be all the better for his presence there. In January, 1910, there was a general election. The sitting member for Canterbury, Sir John Henniker Heaton (as a result of whose great crusading spirit this country once knew the benefits of an imperial penny post) was expected not to stand again, and the perspicacious Goldney planned to take his place. The leading Tories in the constituency were, however, unprepared to accept him as their candidate, and they persuaded Sir John to reconsider his decision. In consequence Canterbury was the scene of one of those internecine struggles which are a recurring phenomenon in British politics. Goldney stood as an Independent Unionist against the official Conservative candidate.

The election was fought with a savage acrimony. The gentry were determined that they should never be represented in Parliament by this thrusting newcomer, while the townspeople believed that, in Goldney, they had found a champion who would put in their deserved places those Tories who had for far too long regarded the constituency as their own especial preserve. When the poll was declared Sir John Henniker Heaton had retained the seat by 21 votes. In the following December, following the death of King Edward and the accession of King George v, there was another general election. This time Sir John could not be persuaded to fight again; and the official Tory candidate was John Howard of Sibton Park. Goldney stood once more as an Independent Unionist, and this time a Liberal candidate also appeared. As a result, Goldney was elected by a majority of 473 votes. He was to retain the seat until his death.

His incursions into the public life of Canterbury were to cause a long lasting split between those who supported him and those who had opposed him. Goldney and his devoted mother were resolutely cut by many of his constituents. As the writer of his obituary notice in the *Kentish Gazette* observed:

> The social conditions amid which he and those dear to him found themselves after the establishment of their residence at Canterbury were not, it must in justice be conceded, such as to bring the best out of a man.

So he set out to impress those who so clearly disliked him. An example of his methods is to be found in the curious story of Giovanni Francesco Romanelli's picture *The Descent from the Cross*.

In 1906 the members of the Committee of the Beaney Institute received from Goldney a printed letter bearing the address of Woburn Abbey, the seat of the Duke of Bedford. This announced that His Grace was generously presenting to the Institute a large oil painting by this distinguished seventeenth-century Italian artist. Goldney made it clear that the gift was worth a great deal of money. The Committee accepted the picture with gratitude and hung it in the Library over a gilt label bearing the inscription, '*Given by His Grace the Duke of Bedford*'. There it remained, respectfully admired by almost all who saw it, until shortly after Goldney was elected as a Member of Parliament.

Coming to see Mr Mead one day he demanded to know who was responsible for placing this legend beneath the picture. Much astonished, the librarian replied that the label had been designed and paid for by Goldney himself. For once a soft answer failed to turn away wrath; and, in a passion of anger, Goldney denied that he had ever done such a thing or had ever, until that morning, read the inscription. It must be altered at once. So, for another six or seven years, the picture hung above a notice recording the generosity of Francis Bennett-Goldney, M.P., who had presented it to the Institute.

At their first meeting after this incident, one of the Committee, Mr Stone, asked who was the actual owner of the picture. At the next, Goldney produced a letter which he said was from the Duke of Bedford, though no one was allowed to peruse it. This stated that the picture belonged to Goldney, who might dispose of it in any way he pleased.

Also in 1906 it was decided to remove to the strong-room in the Beaney Institute the city archives which had till then been stored for safety in the cathedral. Goldney, both as Mayor and Honorary Curator of the Museum, superintended the transfer of these important documents. Seated in his carriage he watched the chests and deed boxes being loaded into the van which was to convey them to the Institute, and he allowed his coachman to lend a helping hand in their removal.

Upon the publication of the Commission of Inquiry's report in Dublin, Mr Stone wrote to the local press pointing out the curious coincidence that there should be in the Bedford Tower one Garter which had belonged to the great Duke of Marlborough, and another, lent by Mr Bennett-Goldney and also said to have belonged to that warrior duke, in the Beaney Institute. According to Mr Stone's account, the publication of his letter caused the immediate removal of the Garter from its case in the museum; but this is not confirmed by entries in the Loans Book of the Institute or the Minute Book of the Committee. These showed that the Garter was lent to the Institute on 2nd November, 1906, and remained there until Mr Mead handed it over with other exhibits to Goldney's executors.

When, upon the outbreak of the First German War, Goldney offered the Miss Russells' house to the nation for use as a hospital, he went to live in Sandgate. Now he was even busier than ever; for in addition to his parliamentary duties he was appointed principal organiser of ambulance services in Kent. It was while driving in connection with these humanitarian interests that he was involved in a motor accident, as a result of which he suffered a renal haemorrhage. Even then, however, he did not feel that he had discharged his duties to the nation; and he continued to seek a more active part in the war effort.

In October, 1917, his efforts were crowned with success. He was appointed Honorary Military Attaché at the British Embassy in Paris. There must, in the autumn of 1917, have been many officers with more adequate claims to be considered for so agreeable a post! In the following June, however, Goldney had a recurrence of the trouble caused by his motor accident, and he was sent to the American Hospital at Brest. On 21st June he wrote to a friend in Canterbury that *'everything will be all right'*. This, according to the *Kentish Gazette*, reflected 'the characteristic cheery assurance', which was typical of Mr Goldney, though it must be said that this side of his character had been in eclipse upon that evening when Shackleton and his 'family lawyer' arrived in Canterbury. However that may be, Francis Bennett-Goldney died on 27th July, 1918.

It would have given him considerable satisfaction to know that, at his funeral at St Germain-en-Laye, the British Ambassador and his staff were his mourners, and that M. Clemenceau was represented at the service. He would also have been surprised if he could have seen how even those Canterbury papers which had consistently opposed him now put away their long and bitter antagonism and spoke in generous terms of the very real services he had rendered to his constituents.

In the following year the first part of his collections was sent for sale by his executors. After Goldney's treasures had reached the sale-rooms of Messrs Puttick and Simpson, the auctioneers notified the Town Clerk of Canterbury, Mr Henry Fielding, that a number of important charters and civic documents relating to Canterbury were to be included in the sale, and they thought it possible that the Town Council would be glad to acquire these for their archives.

Mr Fielding and Mr Stone at once arranged to visit London and examine these records. By a curious coincidence, which must have resulted from a somewhat similar letter having been sent to the Duke of Bedford, His Grace's lawyers were ushered into Puttick and Simpson's store while the gentlemen from Canterbury were examining the documents they had come to see. Hearing who the new arrivals were, and hoping to satisfy himself at last as to the real ownership of the Romanelli hanging in the Institute, Mr Stone approached the lawyers and told them what he knew about the picture. They had no knowledge of it; but, a few days later, Mr Stone received a peremptory letter demanding the return of the Duke's picture and stating that, until this could be arranged, it must be insured for £6,000. The Committee of the Institute at once took steps to send the picture to the Duke of Bedford's lawyers although, understandably, they refused to do anything about insuring it.

As for the Canterbury charters and documents, the Corporation was forced to sue Goldney's executors for the return of their historic archives. The dispute came before the High Court in February, 1921; and it was chiefly due to Mr Mead's evidence that the Corporation won its case. The librarian had been present when the charters and other documents were removed from the Cathedral; and he remembered that, when the boxes were being loaded into the van, he had seen Goldney's coachman place several documents in the Mayor's carriage. The Corporation won back its muniments but was faced with a bill for legal expenses amounting to £500.

It is, perhaps, fitting that we should close this account with a comment on Goldney made by Vicars in a letter to Mr Fuller of 6th July, 1909:

> I do not suspect Goldney for he had no opportunity of access to the safe or any key as S. had – & was only once in Dublin (for 3 days in May) in the year of the robbery. Besides Goldney has money & is a wealthy fellow. . . .

CHAPTER FOUR

Whether or not Richard Gorges played any leading part in the theft of the Irish Crown Jewels, it is certain that he deserves our sympathy as do all born before their time. Poor Gorges was a delinquent without a single psychiatrist to explain his faults if not to curb his excesses. He can never have known much parental love. The son of a lieutenant-colonel in the Indian Army, he was shipped off to South Africa at the age of fourteen when detected in some precocious sexual malpractice. Unusually tall for his age, he found little difficulty in passing himself off as older than he really was. He enlisted in the Cape Mounted Police, and learnt to live hard and to drink hard. Yet in these years he probably experienced a contentment which would, afterwards, always elude him. He was to cling pathetically, throughout his later, seedy years, to the reputation he had once gained of being an all-round sportsman. Gorges was, to use accurately a description which is all too often misplaced, 'a man's man.'

In 1900 he was serving in the South African War with Scott's Border Scouts, and two years later was gazetted captain in the 3rd Battalion, Royal Irish Regiment. For his services in South Africa he was awarded the Queen's Medal with five clasps and the King's Medal with two clasps. He was appointed Regimental Instructor of Musketry in April 1904, as a consequence of which he was posted to Ireland.

Whether or not Gorges and Shackleton met first in South Africa or in Ireland, it is scarcely surprising that these two, with their mutual interest in the unspeakable, should become friends. Nor is it likely that Gorges' reappearance in his native country would pass so unnoticed that old stories regarding the reasons for his youthful departure to South Africa would not have been revived and embellished. Thus it came about that, when Peirce O'Mahony returned to champion Vicars' cause, he would have suggested to his Nationalist friends that Shackleton and Gorges were both more credible stealers of the Irish Crown Jewels than was his own half-brother. Not that O'Mahony was the only one to suspect them, for they must have been the two abandoned ruffians of whom Birrell spoke; but one wonders why O'Mahony never accused Gorges openly, as he did Shackleton, if he sincerely believed him to have been implicated in the theft. For there are certain fragments of evidence which tend to suggest that Gorges may well have known something about the crime.

In Vicars' letter to Mr Fuller of 6th July 1909 is an interesting reference to Gorges:

> Capt. Gorges was in Dublin on 30th June and was a great friend of S's and hand in glove with him. I had refused to allow Gorges into my house for fully a year before the robbery and warned S. that I considered him morally a bad lot and to have nothing to say to him. Gorges was never in the Office to my knowledge for over a year before the robbery and I don't see how he could have got in to do the job after Office Hours. Shackleton, of course, could have gone there any time and, if seen could have said that he had come only for his letters. . . . Of course it is easy to be wise after the event, but who on earth would have guessed that Shackleton or Gorges were perhaps plotting a robbery?

It will be remembered that, after Vicars had returned to Dublin from Abbots Barton, he told Kerr that he believed the theft had taken place on Sunday, 30th June. This, one would think, must have been connected in his mind with the knowledge that Gorges had been in Dublin on that date. Yet, so far as we know, Vicars never said anything to Kane about Gorges being a possible suspect. It can only be said that, if Gorges played any part in the affair, it brought him little benefit.

Dismissed again from the army after the publication of the Report of the Commissioners, he disappeared from the public view until, on August 15th 1911, he was charged at the West London Police Court with obtaining £4 5s. 0d., from the proprietrix of the Baron's Court Hotel, West Kensington, and of obtaining lodging there without paying for it. The money owed was paid before the hearing.

His counsel produced copies of testimonials from a number of distinguished officers testifying to the character of the defendant who, it was stated, had been wounded three times in battle and had been awarded four medals, his last active service having been in the South African War. Nothing was said of the period he had spent as a musketry instructor at Portsmouth and in Ireland.

The magistrate was most sympathetic. Though he told the court that he had no doubt the defendant was guilty of a mean fraud, he went on:

'We do not forget the great obligations we owe to the gallant men who rendered service to the nation when she was in great distress, and I shall set off the public good against the private wrong he has done now. He will be bound over in forty shillings to come up for judgment if called upon.'

Thence Gorges vanished into the long shadows down which a man may creep from West Kensington. Two years later he appeared once more in Ireland. The Volunteer Movement was already beginning to be active and, in Dublin, many Irish nationalists discovered a new zest for living as they laid plans, rational or nonsensical, but for any of which they would gladly have died.

Into this world of cloak and dagger, of tea-parties in Merrion Square and picnics beside the slow-moving waters of the canals, came Richard Gorges with a plan for sale. The years had dealt hardly with him, and drink now played an increasing part in his raffish, ill-conditioned life. But he had no difficulty in finding those among the leaders of the militant Home Rulers who would recognise the potential value of the scheme he had conceived as a result of his rejection by society.

He was finally interviewed, it is said, by Mr Bulmer Hobson, who, in 1908, had written for John Devoy the story of Captain Gaudeans. Recognising his visitor at once, Mr Hobson made up his mind to view with the utmost suspicion all that Gorges might say to him; but they settled down to discuss the plan.

Certainly this possessed the merit of simplicity. The Nationalists were to act upon one of those Bank Holidays which the English keep under even the most adverse circumstances. When the majority of the garrison were off duty and the Government offices closed for the day, the Volunteers should take possession of Dublin Castle. The successful capture of so dramatic an objective would rally all Irish opinion behind the Nationalists, and the British would suffer a crippling blow to their prestige.

Mr Hobson, it is said, listened to his visitor in silence. When Gorges had finished, he thanked him for coming to see him, but explained that the Volunteers could at present serve no more useful purpose than that of irritating the English and providing a focal point for the interest and enthusiasm of the increasing number of freedom-loving Irishmen. They were certainly not yet ready to embark on such a *coup* as Gorges had proposed. Then, as Gorges was about to leave, Mr Hobson restrained him with a seemingly casual remark. 'I've just been reading about you in an American paper, *Gaelic-American*.'

From a drawer beside him he produced his account of Gorges' first departure from the army. As he read this thinly disguised story of Captain Gaudeans, Gorges was convulsed with anger. At last he declared that, if he should ever discover who had written the article, he would have great pleasure in shooting him. On this threatening note they parted and, as the door closed behind Gorges, the author returned the offensive article to his desk.

It cannot be said, however, that Gorges' visit to Dublin bore no fruit. The plans for the Easter Rising in 1916 bore too close a resemblance to those put forward by Gorges five years earlier for them to have been separately conceived. The Rising was timed for Easter Monday when officials and garrison alike were enjoying themselves at the Fairyhouse Races.

It was not to be upon this high dramatic note that Captain Gorges was to make his bow. With the outbreak of the 1914 War, the ex-soldier saw an opportunity of obtaining employment once again. The authorities were too busy to check the records of all who volunteered to join the army; and, on 5th September, Gorges was commissioned as a captain. But the long years of self-pity and disillusionment, the wasted years in which ambition had withered and only appetites had survived, had deprived Gorges of all usefulness to the community. On 20th January 1915, he once more relinquished his commission.

On 1st June following, he rented two rooms in a house at Mount Vernon in Hampstead. It must have been a difficult time for Gorges. Not only were misguided but patriotic women pressing white feathers upon any man of military age who ventured to appear in civilian clothes; but the hoardings bore constant reminders that THE KING WANTS YOU, even though poor Gorges had been repudiated, with brutal finality, by Queen Victoria, Edward VII and, now, George V. So it was necessary that he should invent a story to explain why he was not wearing uniform. He told his landlord, Charles Thorogood, a professional boxer, that he had recently been invalided out of the army after being gassed. Gorges soon became a well-known figure in the neighbourhood of Mount Vernon, this tall, well-built man who was invariably accompanied by two small dogs. The tradesmen with whom he came in contact looked upon him as a harmless eccentric.

On the morning of 14th July a warrant for his arrest was issued. When Detective Sergeant Askew and Detective Alfred Young went to the house, Gorges was out. They obtained entry to his rooms and took possession of a service revolver and 197 cartridges. When Gorges returned to the house with a haberdasher's young assistant at 6.20 p.m. he had been drinking heavily and, finding his rooms had been searched, he went down angrily to demand an explanation from the landlord. Told that the police had been to see him, he declared that he would shoot stone dead the first detective who laid hands upon him.

At 9.45 Askew and Young returned. Gorges was downstairs in the basement and, as the detectives came into the house, he came up towards them. Sergeant Askew saw he had his hands behind his back, so he told Young to remain where he was and he would himself arrest their man. As Askew came to where Gorges was standing, the latter whipped his hands from behind his back. In one he held a small revolver. Askew immediately closed with him and, in the ensuing struggle, a shot was fired. Detective Young fell to the ground, wounded in the chest. He died before the police surgeon could reach him.

When he was formally charged at the police station, Gorges said to the Inspector: 'Don't call me Captain, for the sake of the Regiment.' Then, replying to the charge, he went on:

'I wish to say it was accidental. It was his fault for having tried to take the revolver from me. I had no more intention of shooting him than of shooting you. I was in liquor.'

At five o'clock next morning he was in a less reasonable frame of mind.

'How many police are there at this station?' he asked.

When told, his latent belligerence showed itself. 'Fifty? Well, I had enough rounds for them.'

He made a pitiable figure when he appeared in court. With

13

unkempt hair and unshaven chin, his hands shaking uncontrol-
lably, he clutched alternately at the rails of the dock or rested
his head upon them. A doctor stated that the prisoner was suffering from chronic alcoholism. Thorogood told how Gorges
always carried a small revolver in his hip pocket. He also said
he had never seen anyone drink as heavily as did Gorges; he
began early in the morning and continued throughout the day.
When in drink, Thorogood said, Gorges would be 'silly in his
habits'. A remark, one feels, that is an outstanding example of
the British genius for understatement.

There was little that could be said for Gorges, except that he
had joined the Cape Mounted Police at the age of fourteen and,
having suffered severe sunstroke, he became gravely excited
after drinking. He was found guilty of manslaughter and sentenced to twelve years' penal servitude. Only once, after this,
does Gorges make a brief and anonymous appearance in the
official records to which we have been given access. On 29th
December 1916, an application was made on behalf of Inspector
Sanders of the C.I.D. for the payment of £7 13s. 7d. expended in
going to interview two convicts then serving terms of imprisonment. The explanation given must refer to Gorges.

> A convict [this reads] now undergoing sentence made a
> statement to the effect that a fellow convict had often spoken
> to him regarding the larceny of the Dublin Crown Jewels,
> intimating that he was concerned in the theft and could assist
> in their recovery.... As the convicted criminal had been
> associated with certain persons in Dublin at the time of the
> larceny I communicated with the Dublin Metropolitan Police,
> and Chief Inspector Murphy of that Force, who was employed
> in the original investigation, came to London and, with
> Inspector Sanders of this Department, interviewed both con-
> victs and other persons, both in and out of London, and made
> very careful and thorough enquiry without, I regret to say,
> any very good result. Inspector Sanders was engaged in the
> original enquiry with the late Chief Inspector Kane, and was
> acquainted with the facts.[1]

This is the nearest approach to a confession that the police
ever received, and it seems unwise to dismiss it quite so brusquely as did the detectives. We have seen that Gorges did

[1] Home Office File 156, 610/16.

possess, if only occasionally, the ability and vision to plan bold measures, and the ruthlessness engendered by lack of money and the desire to hit back at the world that had disowned him, which would enable him to carry these out. But whether or not Gorges had any actual part in the theft, or knew the identity of the thief or thieves, the police appear to have discounted whatever it was he had to tell them, just as the authorities had discounted the report submitted to them by Chief Inspector Kane.

On the other hand it is quite possible that Gorges, brooding on his misfortunes while in prison, came to believe that he possessed knowledge regarding the fate of the jewels which, if only the police would believe him, might be turned into a key which would open the prison door and allow him to taste again the fruits of freedom. We can never forget how, in the summer of 1962, we spent an afternoon in the company of a former rebel and listened, entranced and bewildered, to his account of how the Jewels were taken from the Castle and of how he and another had waited, identifiable by their bicycles and the cornflowers they had worn, to take the parcelled diamonds from the Stationery Office van in which they had passed the guards and the police. He had told us of the house in the suburbs to which they had taken their loot, and of the secret *cache* which had been prepared in the cellar, and of how the Jewels were finally disposed of to no less a person than Maxim Litvinoff, then furthering the coming of the Russian Revolution by running two junk yards in Ireland. The story we were told was so assured, the details so seemingly circumstantial, that we were almost persuaded of its truth. Only by a slow and peculiarly difficult process of detection were we forced, much against our wills, to demolish our informant's story and to recognise that what had appeared as a satisfactory solution of our mystery was no more than a figment of a mind honestly deluded. And Gorges' confession may well have been of a similar nature.

Of Richard Howard Gorges it remains for us only to draw the attention of our readers to one curious point, which could hold a moral for us all. The man who was declared to be a chronic alcoholic in 1915, and was then sentenced to twelve years' penal servitude, outlived almost all the other characters in this story, surviving on the reluctant generosity of his family until the 1950's.

CHAPTER FIVE

One by one, the black and the white, the poor silly sheep are passing into the shadows. But though Vicars will have heard news of his former friends from time to time, he will probably not have been greatly moved by the disasters which overtook them. For after the first shock of his dismissal had passed, he longed only to discover means by which he might be reinstated as Ulster King of Arms. As the hopes upon which he buoyed himself up were shattered one by one, he became more and more obsessed with the feeling that he was the victim of a calculated persecution in which the King, the Government, the Lord-Lieutenant, his former friends and even Captain Wilkinson all had a part.

For a time he was grateful to remain quietly with his step-brothers at Grange Con or Kilmorna. Soon, however, Vicars decided that, if his crusade for reinstatement was to be prosecuted with proper vigour, he should be in London. He was doing a certain amount of genealogical work for friends who had previously consulted him at the Office of Arms; and he was thinking of starting up a genealogical and heraldic office in London.

One of his principal sympathisers at this time was James Fuller, the official architect of the Church of Ireland, and it was in writing to him, in letters devoted chiefly to genealogical matters, that Vicars felt able to discuss his problems with almost complete candour.

In May 1909, when Vicars had been in London for some time he wrote to Mr Fuller:

> I hope that mean usurper of my Office won't be knighted. It is just like the cheek of a Guardsman to imagine he knows everything. I suppose he would have undertaken to command a battle ship if he got the offer. He actually had to get lessons in heraldry from I. R. Blake & I suppose he is absolutely ignorant of genealogy or ceremonial. Wait until the Unionists come in & I will 'go for' the whole d— lot.

On 26th June he wrote again.

I feel the least I can do is to afford you all the information I may have after your goodness to me & it is no trouble, only interesting to me as I have nothing to do, this infernal Govt. having deprived me of not only my income but of my means of practising my profession. . . .

You ask whether I am doing anything. Of course I am secretly working away, but it is a slow business as I meet with opposition in all directions. Everyone is afraid of their own shadows, & the Govt. especially because they have reason to be afraid &, having blackmailed me, fear I will resort to the same tactics. Well, I could show them up but it won't serve me as everyone fights shy of scandal. The worst of it is my hands are tied in all directions by the King's interference & those who might help me are afraid because in these days most people are snobs & are afraid of offending H.M. All I can say is that their refusing me justice leaves me as a continual thorn in their side, for I shall never cease until I get redress – the scoundrels know that I have right on my side and are afraid.

The Irish Govt. purposely introduced the scandal idea, of the existence of which so far as the Office was concerned there is no truth whatever & I myself don't believe it of anyone or had no knowledge – for the purpose of alarming H.M. & getting him to consent to my removal. Even if Shackleton was a bad lot morally, of which I had no knowledge, it would not make him steal jewellery! By doing so the Police who were the real custodians of the building out of office hours (when the Police admit the robbery must have occurred) get off scot free & the Bd. of Works for their negligence.

Shackleton, when he was suspected, worked the alleged scandal for all he was worth & even blackened his own character! threatening to produce a social scandal & involve high persons – none of whom I even knew.

This is what prevents my getting justice.

I can't ventilate my grievances for the Press & Parliament have both been 'got at' – it only shows the wicked injustice & consequences of blackmail. Shackleton knew the deadly force of the weapon he wielded – but are the Govt. going to encourage such tactics?

Would any sane man court a full public & judicial inquiry if he had anything to fear?

I live in hope that I may by some means get into a Court of Justice & there I shall be safe & have no fears as to the issue. This will come in time & woe betide the Govt. when it does come.

How Burtchaell could act in the mean & low way he has amazes me. I brought him into the Office & he was my assistant for 14 years & I was awfully kind to him, notwithstanding his dreadful infirmity. But for me I believe he would have succumbed in one of the several fits he had in the Office. His ingratitude, when I think of it, makes me shudder – however he can't & won't profit by it in the long run.

I don't believe the Office is doing a big business, it is far more likely that Burtchaell is lying – the Estimates will show.

The curious part of the business is that everyone over here whom I meet or whom others meet & tell me, all sympathise with me, high & low, & all point to the thief, & yet owing to the underhand tactics of the Govt. I am so far helpless in getting justice.

A cabinet Minister[1] the other day told me he suspected the thief & he was right – I would give you his name in confidence – he is the only gentleman in this Govt. of cads. . . .

It was in February 1910 that Vicars first mentioned to Mr Fuller his plan for opening an office in London. He was writing about some genealogical MSS. which the faithful Miss Gibbon was copying for him. Then he continued:

I hope you will not let any of those low blackguards at the Castle have them, but will leave them in your Will to the British Museum, as I hope to do with any MSS. I may have.

I am thinking of starting with a friend an Office in London for genealogical research &c. & if I send out a circular stating who I am & the way in which I was treated

[1] Almost certainly Herbert Gladstone, the Home Secretary.

by the Govt. it will probably produce some sympathy for me & get me work.

It is hard lines for me at my time of life to have to start afresh after one's profession has been purposely shattered by a heartless Govt. But I may not always be poor &, if I can afford it, I shall give trouble to those who have wronged me.

That was the year of King Edward's death and Shackleton's bankruptcy, two events which may have caused Vicars to postpone any decision as to his projected venture. Then, before the year was out, a new anxiety loomed upon his already black horizon. The first reference to this appears in a letter he wrote to Mr Fuller on 9th October:

I have been intending to write to you for some months, but have been away in England & now am rather bothered over a legal case that is coming on. The Irish Govt., goaded on by that Usurper Wilkinson &, I suppose, the grateful Burtchaell, are taking proceedings against me for an obsolete badge – not my Ulster one which I handed over – but another that I have an absolute right to. Its value is only nominal, but on principle I won't give it up. I have suffered enough persecution at the hands of the present Irish Govt. of low cads & I intend to show up their conduct & also to claim the 430 bundles of my MSS. which they retained.

I have entered an appearance & intend to *defend* myself & shall have a holy row. Whatever the result I intend to interest the public!

Mr Fuller at once invited Vicars to stay with him while he was in Dublin for the hearing of the case. In his answer, Vicars recapitulated his reasons for not employing Counsel. He also mentioned an event which may have played a considerable part in making him decide not to open an office in London. Miss Gibbon, who had continued to work for him since his dismissal, had gone to seek her fortune in the United States.

On 28th November *The Times* published a report which stated that:

proceedings had been instituted by the Crown against Sir Arthur Vicars. . . . The information which has been filed . . .

prays for a declaration that the badge of gold provided for the service of the Registrar of the Order of St Patrick, which it is alleged is now in the possession of Sir Arthur Vicars, is the property of the King, and an order is asked for its delivery to the King, or in default damages.

There had been an unfortunate misunderstanding because, on 22nd November, Vicars had sent the badge to the King; but it was not until 10th December that Sir Arthur Bigge, King George's Private Secretary, informed the Home Secretary that the badge had been received.[1]

The Coronation came and went. The King and Queen visited Ireland and there was an investiture of two new Knights of St Patrick. As a consequence, *John Bull* revived the story of the lost Crown Jewels, though the author did not believe they were lost.

> Two years ago *John Bull* stated, and it was never contradicted, that the Jewels stolen from Dublin Castle were worn at the investiture of the Earl of Granard. . . . We are now informed on authority that leaves nothing to be desired that the baubles were again worn at the recent double investiture when His Majesty was on his Irish visit. It is useless to ask in the House where the Jewels were found and by whom they were hypothecated. We were in a position to know all the main facts of how they were taken from the Castle, where they were found, by whom the money was supplied for their release, and the double reward – it was to have been a triple reward if Lord Aberdeen had retired – given to the millionaire who paid for their release. The Dublin Castle officials who are in the know here have been told to inform inquirers that the set of Jewels is a replica recently turned out, but that story will not work. It will be remembered that when the scandal was fresh and the newspapers were inquiring, the detectives announced that they knew the jewels were intact, probably forgetting that the statement was tantamount to an admission that they knew where they were, which they did. Meantime, the Dreyfus of the case, Sir Arthur Vicars, is left by the Government on his Devil's Island, and Nemesis has overtaken several persons whose names were prominently mentioned during the so-called trial. One of them, at least, having fallen on evil times, is hawking around for sale a mass of correspondence that passed between

[1] Home Office File 156, 610/16.

himself and his friends some years ago. It might have been
interesting to newspaper readers when the case was fresh, but
it is useless from the editorial point of view now.

On 12th September, Vicars wrote of this article to Mr Fuller:

> I know nothing about my old Office except that Wilkinson
> is never there & Burtchaell runs the whole show – & has no
> time for anything. I don't suppose I shall get any redress until
> the Unionists come in, when they can't well refuse me. As
> soon as I get any money I shall 'go for them', the low lot of
> blackguards.
>
> Several friends sent me the article in *John Bull*. Of course
> it is all nonsense. I only wish it were true. Pirrie[1] assured me he
> never gave a 1d. for the purpose & was never even approached
> on the subject. He gave this on his word of honour so that I
> could deny it.
>
> At the private investiture of Lord Granard the Undress
> Insignia was worn, which was not stolen, & it was in the day-
> time & so jewelled insignia would not be correct. My nephew
> told me this for he was present. At the Investiture by the King
> he wore his own diamond insignia.
>
> If such jobbery as *John Bull* states were true, it would be
> bound to come out & would be the end of the Govt. at once.
>
> No, I was simply made a scapegoat to save Ross of Bladens-
> burg & the Board of Works, and Shackleton's wicked threats
> of a scandal (which were & are all bunkum & lies) were utilised
> to frighten the late King & make him hush it up. S. was the
> thief & shields himself by threatening blackmail. I can't move
> or get at him & am powerless. . . .
>
> If they gave me a public & judicial inquiry the public would
> soon learn the truth & the saddle be put on the right horse, but
> they are afraid to do this. However, time will surely overtake
> them in their diabolical & unjust tactics.

In September, 1912, George Mahoney died and Kilmorna
passed to Vicars' sister Edith, Mrs de Janasz. She at once
offered Vicars the place, free, for as long as he wished to remain
there. Probably, apart from being reinstated as Ulster King of
Arms, no other single gesture could have done more to soothe Sir
Arthur's anxious heart. Yet he can scarcely have begun to ap-

1 William James Pirrie (1847-1924) Chairman of Harland and Wolff: created
baron 1906; Viscount 1921.

preciate all that life at Kilmorna would mean to him than there
came a new and altogether unexpected blow.

On 11th November 1912, the *London Mail*, a weekly paper of
the most scurrilous kind, specialising in gossip and conjecture
about members of Society, published an extraordinary article.

> What happened [demanded the writer] in Dublin Castle the
> night before the Crown Jewels were stolen? And why the lady
> who carried out such an elaborate scheme of revenge against
> Sir Arthur Vicars was allowed to go unpunished? Further,
> what led Sir Arthur Vicars to shield this lady, and that at the
> cost of his post and his honour, and what return the lady made
> him for this sacrifice? And why those officials, all enjoying the
> highest posts in the Irish Administration, had remained mute
> through the whole affair, allowed the word 'robbery' to be
> bruited about and yet all the time knew that the jewels were
> never off the Castle premises? And as a last query, that wants
> a great deal of explaining: Why did Lord and Lady Aberdeen
> display such extraordinary and inhuman vindictiveness against
> Sir Arthur Vicars when their son, Lord Haddo, did all he could
> to vindicate the accused man?

> Will any one ever have the courage to tell the whole truth
> about this wretched business, revolving as it has round love,
> jealousy and a culminating tragedy of fiendish revenge?

There was nothing Vicars could do but issue a writ claiming
damages for libel; and those responsible for the publication of
the offending article were summoned to appear on 14th January
1913, when a stated claim was delivered by Vicars' lawyers. Two
possible courses were now open to the defendants. They could
stand by all they had written and published; or they could admit
that they had been misled and published material they were now
persuaded was false. In the latter case they would be expected to
publish ample apologies and offer Vicars amends of any reasonable nature that he cared to ask. The editor of the paper Mr A.
Moreton Mandeville, chose the former course; and Vicars'
lawyers at once asked that Mr Mandeville should produce Particulars of Justification stating the grounds upon which he
would base his defence. When these were presented on 31st
March, Vicars reading them, must have felt that he had been
translated into a nightmare world.

The chief points of this extraordinary document were that
a key of the safe, or a skeleton copy, had been obtained by a

woman 'going by the name of Malony and commonly known as Molly, but who is now known by the name of Madame Robinson.' This lady, it was stated, 'had acted as and was in fact the mistress of the plaintiff.' The Particulars then continued:

It is the fact that shortly before the removal of the said jewels the plaintiff had become and was on terms of great intimacy and friendship with one Lady Haddo, the daughter-in-law of Lord Aberdeen, the late Viceroy of Ireland. The said woman Malony or Molly was greatly incensed at and became very jealous of the said intimacy and friendship.

It is the fact that on the night previous to the removal of the said jewels there were visitors to Dublin Castle, amongst others being the said woman, Malony or Molly, Lord Sutherland Gower [*sic*] and Mr Shackleton, and it is the fact that the said last named persons were playing cards with the plaintiff on the said night. At the end of the said game of cards the plaintiff retired with and occupied the same bed during the night with the said woman.

It is the fact that the said woman left Dublin Castle unperceived by the occupants of the Castle in the early hours of the next morning and it is the fact that the plaintiff did not attempt to detain her there or prevent her from so leaving. The plaintiff directly or indirectly supplied to the said woman the means necessary to enable her to escape to Paris.

It is the fact that the plaintiff concealed and suppressed from the Commissioners which sat to inquire into the loss of the said jewels the circumstances of the night previous to the removal of the said jewels, and the fact that the said woman had occupied the same bed with him as aforesaid and the fact that at some time or times she had acted as and been his mistress.

Three months elapsed. Then, on 4th July 1913, the case was heard in the King's Bench Division before Mr Justice Darling and a special jury. Once again Vicars was represented by Mr Campbell, K.C., who was supported this time by Mr Cohen. Mr Montague Shearman appeared for the *London Mail*.

No sooner had Mr Campbell risen to open the case than Mr Shearman interrupted him in order to make an astonishing statement: that he had already told Mr Campbell that no attempt would be made to justify anything which appeared in the article.

Mr Campbell was not to be placated. After saying that he had only been informed that morning of the instructions now given to Mr Shearman, he pointed out that the *London Mail* claimed an enormous circulation, and that the offensive article, a monstrous edifice of lies, had appeared close on eight months earlier. He then proceeded to read both the article and the Particulars of Justification and, at the end, said there was no warrant for a single statement in this accumulation of filth and disgusting detail. He drew the attention of the Court to the suffering caused to Lady Haddo as well as to Sir Arthur Vicars; and he stated that both Lord and Lady Haddo had travelled from Ireland to deny the whole fabrication. He hoped Mr Shearman's clients would get no pity from the jury, for no one would know what a life of misery and suffering the plaintiff had gone through during these last years.

Vicars, Lord Haddo and Lady Haddo gave evidence in turn that there was no word of truth in the article or in the Particulars of Justification. During Lady Haddo's evidence it transpired that she had only met Vicars once, 'in a casual way, at a public function'. The case for Vicars then being concluded, Mr Shearman announced that he did not intend to call any evidence as the story published by his clients was a complete myth. The defendants were satisfied that the woman Malony or Madame Robinson did not exist.

In his summing up Mr Justice Darling described the *London Mail* as a paper concerned only in vulgar fashion with the doings of various people; it did not contain anything of value as news. He went on to describe as most offensive the suggestions made concerning Lady Haddo and Sir Arthur Vicars. After which it is scarcely surprising that the jury took only nine minutes to decide that the libel had been proved. Vicars was awarded damages of five thousand pounds.

Although, in 1913, this sum represented a very considerable addition to his funds, he can have gained little satisfaction as a result of the case being brought. He had always said, since his dismissal, that, if he could find himself in a court of law, he would be able to air his grievances and, perhaps, prove his complete blamelessness for the theft of the jewels; but Mr Campbell, perspicaciously, had contrived to prevent this. Also, Vicars was a kindly man, and he must have hated the thought of the anxiety and shrinking distaste which Lady Haddo must have experienced as a result of the *London Mail*'s attack upon herself and him. Both Lord and Lady Haddo had behaved extremely well towards him; and there can be no doubt that, had she chosen also to sue the *London Mail*, she must have been awarded very heavy damages.

Perhaps nothing in this story is more baffling than the behaviour on this occasion of Mr Moreton Mandeville. He must have known exactly what constituted a published libel; yet he persisted, until the very day of the hearing, to say that he would substantiate the statements made in his Particulars of Justification. Yet it is unlikely that Mr Mandeville was a philanthropist anxious only to provide impoverished Vicars with a certain amount of capital.

The whole incident is inexplicable unless some unnamed person, anxious for one reason or another to make provision for Vicars in his need, persuaded Mr Mandeville that he would pay whatever damages might be awarded to Vicars and, if necessary, to Lady Haddo, as well as all legal expenses and, it is to be presumed, a not insignificant sum to Mandeville himself for his services in this matter. All of which suggests that Vicars' anonymous benefactor was a very rich man.

Peirce O'Mahony, by that time The O'Mahony of Kerry, is the obvious candidate for this philanthropic post, a man who had constantly proved his readiness to disburse large sums of money for the benefit of those whom he regarded as victims of one kind or another; but he may have found, or known, that Vicars' pride, his continuing wish to live according to the pattern he believed had been evolved by his eighteenth-century forebears, would make it impossible for him to accept a gift of actual money. (Board and lodging at Grange Con, the use of Kilmorna for the rest of his life: these were acceptable benefits which fell conveniently into a different category from a capital sum.) It has been objected that Peirce O'Mahony was, above all else, an Irish gentleman and, as such, could never have formed a plan which would bring a lady's name and honour into disrepute.[1]

[1] It has to be admitted that Lady Haddo did not always rouse the most chivalrous instincts in men. The Editor of *The Complete Peerage* (Vol. I, p. 18) inserted a quite unnecessary footnote to point out that, at the time of her first marriage, to 'a partner in a very flourishing drapery business', Lord Haddo, her second husband, was only two years old.

It is improbable that the eccentric Mr Wallace, who had evidently felt very keenly that Vicars had been the victim of malice, would have chosen such a way to put things right, even if he could have afforded to do so. He believed, with a persistence that was more pathetic than sensible, that he would eventually gain Vicars' reinstatement through the process of the law. And, if the involved plan we have suggested was followed by someone who was neither O'Mahony nor Wallace, then it would appear that some other person of wealth felt he must make what amends he could for all that Vicars had suffered, and this person will have felt no compunction about dragging Lady Haddo's name through the courts. It is completely baffling.

There is, however, one tenuous hint that Vicars himself may have inspired this extraordinary affair. In a letter he wrote to Mr Fuller on 6th July 1909, is this passage:

> If I brought an action tomorrow Birrell, Aberdeen and Co. would claim privilege. I cannot understand why the Almighty has not overtaken these blackguards and enabled me to triumph over the brutes, but it may come yet. The interference of the King did for me and so far has withheld justice. If you want to aid me, you will try to get someone to slander me to you and thus enable me to get into a court of law when I can bring the whole thing out.

The verdict in the libel action prompted Peirce O'Mahony and Vicars to renew their appeals to the Government. On 14th July, the former sent a petition to Mr Birrell. In this he wrote:

> The verdict of a British Jury in favour of my brother, Sir Arthur Vicars, seems to me to present a favourable opportunity of once more appealing to you to reconsider the harsh and unfair treatment meted out to him by the Irish Government. . . . A secret inquiry was set on foot by the Irish Government and a report furnished to his late Majesty King Edward, including most baseless insinuations against my brother's character. My brother from that day to this has never been informed of the contents of that report, nor of the exact character of those insinuations.

Then, after recapitulating the story of the theft, the offer of a

pension to Vicars and the proceedings of the Commission of
Inquiry, O'Mahony continued:

> My brother was deprived of his office, financially ruined
> and, as far as the Government could compass it, deprived
> of all opportunity of defending his character. Smarting
> under a deep sense of resentment, at what I considered &
> still consider the cruel & most unjust treatment of my
> brother, I used expressions regarding your personal con-
> duct in the matter, which, on calmer reflection, I con-
> sidered were not justified, and for which I subsequently
> expressed to you my regret.... The Government succeeded
> in making my brother's life for the past six years a verit-
> able hell upon earth. I cannot believe that that was the
> deliberate intention either of His Excellency or you, still
> less can I believe that it was the intention of His late
> Majesty. My brother in the eyes of the Government de-
> served a pension in October 1907.... If then he deserved a
> pension, he deserves one far more now....
>
> I appeal to you now even at the eleventh hour to do
> some small modicum of justice to my brother, and at least
> to secure for him that pension which you were willing to
> give him in 1907.... [1]

On 31st July, Vicars petitioned Lord Aberdeen to forward to
King George his prayer for the setting up of a new Commission
of Inquiry. On 14th August, Sir James Dougherty, acting on the
instructions of Birrell, forwarded the petition to the Home
Secretary with the following comment:

> The Chief Secretary would therefore humbly submit for
> His Majesty's consideration that the Prayer of the Petition
> is not one that can be complied with.

The papers were laid before the King, who was at Balmoral,
on 22nd August. With characteristic directness, His Majesty instructed Lord Stamfordham to write immediately to the Under-
Secretary of State at the Home Office in these terms:

> The King cannot help thinking that it is a pity not to
> grant Sir A. Vicars' Petition for a Public Inquiry, where
> the witness would be examined on oath.

[1] These and the related papers are in Home Office File 156/610/16.

In His Majesty's opinion nothing should be left undone which might possibly lead to the recovery of the Jewels.

This was forwarded to the Home Secretary, Mr Reginald McKenna; and, to the covering letter which accompanied it, was an interesting postscript added by one of the Under-Secretaries.

I think there ought to be legislation to enable Royal or Viceregal Commissions generally to take evidence on oath, but the present occasion is a bad one for proposing it.

Mr McKenna wrote to Lord Stamfordham on 30th August.

. . . I think perhaps I had better state the reasons present to my mind when I submitted the petition to His Majesty. Firstly, to hold a new inquiry with sworn evidence would require express legislation for the purpose; secondly, to adopt such a course would be contrary to the advice of the Chief Secretary, who points out that, when the former inquiry was held by a properly constituted Commission, S⁻ Arthur Vicars refused to give evidence or to assist the proceedings in any way; and, thirdly, there is nothing in the Petition to suggest that a new inquiry would yield any result as regards the recovery of the Crown Jewels.

These reasons are cogent, and appear to me to justify a refusal of the petition. If, however, His Majesty thinks that a new inquiry with sworn evidence might be of value, I will communicate with the Prime Minister as to the prospect of the time being available in the next Session of Parliament for the necessary legislation.

So King George's wish to undo, at least to some extent, the injustice done to Vicars by his royal father's dread of unsavoury publicity, and at the same time to make a belated attempt to trace the missing jewels, was smothered in governmental red tape. Yet, in submitting to the pressures which radiated from Dublin Castle, Lord Stamfordham indicated that His Majesty was not altogether happy about the decision reached by his advisers.

The King does not wish to press for a new inquiry with sworn evidence into the loss of the Irish Crown Jewels.

His Majesty's only desire was that even now at this distance of time nothing should be left undone to recover the stolen property.

And not until the end of the month did the Irish authorities remember to inform Vicars that his petition had been disallowed.

In the year which followed, Vicars began at last to regain the peace of mind which had forsaken him when the Crown Jewels were stolen. He had always loved Kilmorna; and now he continued the work George Mahony had done in beautifying the gardens and policies. He had already done much to improve the interiors of those Protestant churches in Dublin and its neighbourhood which might be described as 'High Anglican', and he now presented to his parish church at Listowel a brass lectern in memory of George Mahony, and brought over from England some ancient choir-stalls and other decorative objects.

Then, little more than a year after the libel action, came the shattering news of young Peirce Mahony's death and, immediately after that, the declaration of war between Great Britain and Germany. Through the years which followed, Vicars did all he could to aid the war effort and, in the course of this patriotic work, became keenly interested in the Boy Scout movement and was made honorary secretary to the Listowel Association. After the Easter Rising in 1916, Ireland became an armed camp; and life at Kilmorna proved increasingly lonely for the man who had once presided over the ceremonial pageantry of the Viceregal Court.

Then, in 1917, Vicars surprised his friends by marrying his old friend Miss Gertrude Wright, the elder sister of Peirce Mahony's widow. Vicars was now fifty-three; and if, as many have suggested, he was a homosexual, his marriage deserves to be quoted as an encouraging example of the triumph of persistence over propensity. Lady Vicars did much, despite her husband's increasing ill-health, to erase from his mind any bitterness which survived from the events of 1907.

Life in Ireland was becoming more and more difficult; but the Vicars continued to do all they could to help their less fortunate neighbours. Many times Sir Arthur was warned that he must not show friendliness towards the Government-controlled

14

police or the British troops stationed in the district. But he
could not be persuaded to give up his habit of taking these men
presents of fruit from the Kilmorna gardens.

'We shall be all right,' he told his over-anxious friends.
'Nobody will do anything against us.'

He still retained his old ability to ignore those things he had
no wish to recognise; but the men and women whose names had
figured in the lists he once prepared for the Lord Lieutenant
were leaving Ireland now, if they were not shot before their
burning homes.

The days of British domination in Ireland were passing. Time
was running out; and, when the end came, as soon it must,
there would be no room in the new Ireland for such as Arthur
Vicars, who looked back still to the great days of English rule in
Dublin, the last years before the union of the Parliaments, as
to a golden millennium.

On 6th May 1920, Lord Askwith rose in the House of Lords
to intervene in a debate on Irish affairs. He held a letter written
in the bold and flowing hand of the former Ulster King of Arms.
Lord Askwith read to his fellow peers Vicars' description of a
night raid made upon Kilmorna by a force of about a hundred
armed men. Fortunately Lady Vicars had been away on a visit
to friends. Hearing a loud knocking on the front door, Sir
Arthur had asked who wished to see him. In reply he was ordered
to open the door. This he refused to do and, as the raiders
broke down the door, he remained standing in the hall, resolute
and alone. Then, as the men forced their way in, their leader
ordered Vicars to hand over the keys of the strong-room. He
refused. Thereupon ten men lined up facing him. On an order
they brought their rifles to their shoulders. Slowly the leader
counted: one ... two ... three. There he paused and again asked
Vicars for his keys. Once more Vicars refused, but he agreed to
show them where the strong-room was. After strenuous but
vain efforts to break down the door, the men left the house.
Vicars had shown himself to possess courage of a quality which,
at any other time, would have gained immediate recognition
from men of Irish blood and Irish birth.

Nearly another year of dark and bloody deeds succeeded this
outrage. Then, on the morning of 14th April 1921, Vicars, who
had been ill, was still in bed when the manager of the estate

came to see him on business. While they were talking, Lady
Vicars joined them.

'There are men with pistols in their hands round the house,'
she told them.

'I went to the window,' the manager said later, 'and saw two
men, each carrying two revolvers. I told Sir Arthur to get
dressed at once, and went downstairs to secure the doors. Two
of the raiders were near the back doors talking to the valet and
the cook. One of these men said, 'It is all right, we have come
only to burn the house'. I replied that I was sorry, but that I
hoped no lives would be taken. He replied that he would guarantee that no lives would be lost, and held out his hand to me.
He told me to get out of the house, and that I only had two
minutes more to do so. I again rushed upstairs to Sir Arthur's
room and found him and Lady Vicars together. I told them
what the raiders' intentions were. At his request, I collected the
various valuable possessions of his and took them down, and
placed them outside the front door. I was ascending the stairs to
the third floor for the third time when I was stopped by one of
the raiders who had a revolver in his hand, and who ordered me
down stairs, where he placed me under guard. . . .'

Sir Arthur's valet, whose father was a gardener at Kilmorna,
said it had been 10 a.m. when he heard a crash of glass and went
to the kitchen to see what had happened. He saw a man in the
long hall with a bandage around his forehead. The stranger had
pointed a double-barrelled gun at him and then disappeared.
The cook, greatly distressed, came up to the witness and, as she
was on the verge of fainting, he took her into the yard. There
they met a man with a revolver, who said that it was intended to
burn the house, but that nothing would happen to them. He
asked the man if he could go into the house and bring out Sir
Arthur. The man consented, and gave him two minutes in which
to do so.

'The house was then burning,' continued the valet, 'and I
informed Sir Arthur of this fact . . . At the time he was in his
dressing-gown, having just got up. I helped him to save some of
his property by throwing it out of the window. He told me
then to go to the dining-room to save the pictures of Mr
O'Mahony, his brother, and Lady Rossmore and some others.
This I did by putting them through the window. I then returned

to Sir Arthur and told him that the house was well alight, and that he had better come out at once. We both left the house together, Sir Arthur going by the front terrace.'

The manager took up the story.

'This man (who had placed me under guard) asked me who had gone down the terrace steps, and someone replied, 'That is Sir Arthur'. This man, accompanied by three or four others, immediately went after him. I heard Sir Arthur say a few words, and immediately after several revolver shots rang out. I was still held prisoner. Presently another leader of the raiders returned with a party and ordered me to the front of the house, and told me to go down to the trees. At that moment a cloud of smoke from the burning house came across our path, and I took advantage of it in order to get away. I ran down the terrace and, on getting clear of the smoke, I saw Sir Arthur's body lying at the foot of the steps on the round terrace. I did not stop as I believed they intended to murder me also. I hid in a plantation for about three-quarters of an hour, and then returned to the burning building, near which I found Lady Vicars and others.'

After the valet had left Sir Arthur, he had gone through the dining-room and kitchen and joined Lady Vicars and the cook in the kitchen yard. Immediately afterwards he had heard shots and, as soon as the raiders left, he went in search of his employer and found his body at the foot of the lowest terrace in front of the house. He then got in touch with the military, who arrived just after midday.

The following announcement was issued from Dublin Castle that evening:

> Sir Arthur Vicars of Kilmorna House was taken from his bed in his dressing-gown this morning and murdered outside his house. A label was placed around his neck with the words, '*Spy. Informers beware. I.R.A. never forgets.*' The house and contents were afterwards fired and completely destroyed. About 30 armed men participated.

Speaking in the House of Commons on 19th April, Mr Lloyd George quoted an article which had appeared in the *Manchester Guardian* after Vicars' death. The writer described his murder as:

> One of the most horrible in the black recent records of crime and counter crime in Ireland. For a crowd of armed men to

attack an unarmed man in a lonely house, take him out of bed and jointly murder him, they must have debauched their minds with the base casuistry of 'a state of war', to an extent which makes them a curse to any cause they pretend to honour.

Even in Ireland, long grown accustomed to tales of murder and sudden death, the news of Vicars' end made a profound impression. Men and women, pledged to the cause of Irish liberty, remembered the treatment he had received at the hands of the British Government; and, even though they knew he had not supported their own aspirations, they could not believe that he had ever been actively against them. The I.R.A. took the almost unprecedented step of announcing that the murder had not been carried out by its orders.

Although, at the inquiry held after the murder, the various witnesses all declared that they had never seen any of the raiders before, it was generally accepted that the destruction of the house and the murder of Vicars had been the work of local men. As a result, when the Treaty was signed and the Free State Government instituted their agrarian policy of dividing up the large estates among the local people, the authorities refused to allow any local man to obtain possession of any part of the Kilmorna estate. Thus did they signalise their regret that one who had loved Ireland, even though it was not their Ireland, should have been killed by Irishmen in the name of liberty.

POSTSCRIPT

That we should have attempted, fairly early in our enquiries, to discover what were the contents of Sir Arthur Vicars' Will was due to no thought that that document might contain any reference to the Irish Crown Jewels. We just regarded it as one of the more obvious ways in which we might gain a more complete insight into Vicars' character. We raised the question in two widely separated sources of information and in both we drew a blank. In one we were told that, if Vicars had made a will, it almost certainly perished in the fire which consumed Kilmorna. In the other it was suggested that this Will, along with many others, was lost in the fire which destroyed the Four Courts in Dublin during the Civil War. It seemed reasonably certain that the Will no longer existed, if in fact it ever did. We had, at that time, not fully appreciated how all-enveloping was the cloak of secrecy and evasion with which the facts of the case would be shrouded. With so many avenues to explore, we may be forgiven for having supposed that this was one we could regard as closed.

It was therefore with mixed feelings that, when the preceding chapters were already in the printers' hands, we received a copy of Vicars' Will. So unexpected is one of its passages, so odd the new mystery it contains, we felt we must make this short addition to our book.

After making a number of personal and charitable bequests, Vicars continued :-

'I have purposely not bequeathed any legacy to my half brother Peirce Charles de Lacy Mahony styling himself The O'Mahony because I know he has left nothing to me by his Will and also because he got from my wife at the time of my marriage and unknown to me (I don't think he or she is aware that I know of it even now) the sum of £300 to pay costs incurred by him over my case at the time of the Inquiry concerning the loss of the Crown Jewels and concerning the conduct of which inquiry I had no voice whatever and owing to my said brother's then action I refused the offer of a pension from the Government at my said brother's promise to provide me with an equivalent. This he subsequently repudiated although his own Solicitor admitted that he had pledged himself to do so. For the same reason I abrogate the undertaking I gave to repay the sum of about £500 which my said brother advanced to me at that time as I regarded it to have been got from me under misconception and uncommonly like fraud. And I know that his son Dermot Mahony will not claim it.'

Upon our first reading of this passage we felt a sense of horrified incredulity. How could Vicars, that kindly and considerate person who always attempted to present himself in the character of a man of taste and breeding, publish such an indictment of the stepbrother upon whose charity he had lived for years? Had those peaceful years at Kilmorna brought to him nothing but an aggravation of bitterness and self-pity? As to the story of what The O'Mahony may or may not have done, that Vicars had not the courage to broach the subject to his wife suggests that his view of the matter may have been based entirely upon a misunderstanding of what had really taken place. Granted that both men were extremely difficult, self-opinionated, obstinate and proud, thus making it even more difficult than usual for either to establish a good relationship with the other, whether as benefactor or beneficiary, it seems highly unlikely that The O'Mahony behaved quite in the way which Vicars suggests. If The O'Mahony did repudiate his promise to provide his step-brother with an equivalent to the pension offered to the latter by the Government, we are inclined to believe that he did so only after Vicars had made it impossible for him to do so in a frank and open way so that The O'Mahony, determined to carry out his side of the bargain despite Vicars' hurt feelings, had been forced to conspire with Mr Moreton Mandeville in the elaborate farce which culminated in Vicars being awarded five thousand pounds damages for libel. It is quite understandable that, having taken that course, The O'Mahony would have found it impossible to tell his stepbrother what he had done.

A clue to Vicars' behaviour may be found in the date upon which he signed his Will. This was on 14th May, 1920, eight days after Lord Askwith had read to his fellow peers Vicars' account of the first raid on Kilmorna. That incident, sufficient to shake the equanimity of any man, may well have disturbed his mind to such an extent that whereas, previously, all Vicars' feelings of bitterness had been directed against those in authority whom he regarded as his persecutors, they now became concentrated against his brother.

Another question that clamours for explanation is why the executors of the Will, Lady Vicars, his brother Major Vicars and his sister Mrs de Janasz, should have allowed this passage to be admitted to probate. Did all of them wish to drag into public the unhappy relations existing, at least in Vicars' mind, between him and his distinguished brother? It was certainly not because they understood that everything written in a Will must needs be admitted to Probate. On 1st March, 1922, they signed the necessary Oath for Executors and when, on 22nd March, it was admitted for Probate in the High Court of Justice in Southern Ireland, the following note, preceded by an asterisk, was affixed at its foot.

'By direction of the Rt Honble Mr Justice Dodd let the words beginning "I might have had" (line 36 p. 2) to the words "the next world" (line 8, p. 3) be excluded from probate, E. H. Kenny, Registrar, 20/3/22.

The original Will now reposes in a sealed envelope in the Records Office in Dublin bearing the injunction, 'Not to be opened without the order of a High Court Judge or of the Principal Probate Registrar', and signed in 1947 by that distinguished Protestant Sinn Feiner, the late Diarmid Coffey, then Deputy Keeper of the Records. Believing that the passage could not have been excluded from Probate if it merely continued the attack upon The O'Mahony, application was made to the present Principal Probate Registrar and to the President of the High Court. Both gentlemen have courteously refused us permission to inspect the original document.

One wonders what it could be that, after nearly forty-four years, must still be shrouded in mystery. Is it that Vicars named the person whom he believed to have abstracted the Crown Jewels from the safe and thus set in motion the chain of events which were to bring ruin upon himself and tragedy to so many involved in the story? If this is so, we feel that now, with almost all dead who were in any way connected with the case, the contents of the sealed envelope should be made known.

In closing, however, we would ask our readers not to remember Sir Arthur Vicars as the involuntary recluse of Kilmorna, his mind obsessed by a series of real or imaginary wrongs, but as his memory remained in the hearts and minds of those who knew him well. On 22nd April, 1921, the following lines appeared in the *Church of Ireland Gazette*, under the title, '*In Memoriam–Arthur Vicars, Knight.*'

> Churchman all-knightly, in thy form and mien,
> True fellow with the saintly knights of old,
> Alert and gallant, chivalrous and bold–
> We read it in that brow, those eyes so keen,
> That touch so gentle, that sweet smile serene.
> Thine honour was unsullied, pure as gold;
> Thy courage dauntless, yes, a thousand-fold;
> Thy life, thy worship upright, true and clean.
> And thou wast slain with horror multiplied,
> Like some offending brute led forth and shot
> By ruthless hands, no helper at thy side
> To soothe the anguish of thy soul distraught.
> A land defiled with cruelty and wrong
> Utters its bitter cry: Oh, Lord, how long?

INDEX

INDEX 211